MEDIÆVAL MYSTICAL TRADITION
AND SAINT JOHN OF THE CROSS

life—and shows how this conversation (for all its divergent viewpoints) bore fruit in the profound mystical theology of St John of the Cross. This book is a gift for anyone who seeks historical grounding as well as sound guidance on the pathways from prayer to contemplation.

—**CAROL ZALESKI**, Professor of World Religions at Smith College, author of *The Life of the World to Come*, and co-author with Philip Zaleski of *Prayer: A History*

There is one—and one only—unqualified end of the Church, and that is the union of her members with the triune God. Thus, mystical transformation is the reason proper for the Church's existence. In this admirable volume, the Christian mystical tradition is presented in both its breadth and depth, and in a scholarly and historically sensitive way. It is, in fact, a remarkably clear work about a topic elsewhere often replete with obscurities. John of the Cross is revealed to be to mystical theology what Thomas Aquinas was to theology in general: "God's Goldfinch" is the universal doctor on the subject of mystical transformation. Moreover, far from some gnostic "ascent" of the "inner self" out of the world of experience, Carmelite detachment—the path of "nada"—is one of purification of all in oneself that might mistake creatures for their Creator, so as to really love the former insomuch as they glorify the latter; hence, in his love of nature, John of the Cross is compared herein to Francis of Assisi. Even those well versed in mystical theology will learn plenty from studying this instructive volume.

—**SEBASTIAN MORELLO**, Ph.D., author of *Mysticism, Magic, and Monasteries: Recovering the Sacred Mystery at the Heart of Reality*

Mediæval Mystical Tradition
and
Saint John of the Cross

BY
A BENEDICTINE OF
STANBROOK ABBEY

AROUCA
PRESS

Second Edition © by Arouca Press 2025
Waterloo, ON N2J 0A5
www.aroucapress.com

Originally published by The Newman
Press (Westminster, MD), 1954.

ISBN: 978-1-998492-24-4 (pbk)
ISBN: 978-1-998492-25-1 (hc)

CONTENTS

INTRODUCTION

THE PRESENT MODEST WORK IS NOT intended to add one more to the many books on prayer and the spiritual life, nor is it another biography of St. John of the Cross. It is a study in mediæval and sixteenth-century spirituality and may, perhaps, at least blaze a trail for abler explorers.

One who sets out upon such a quest, however soon discovers that before proceeding far it is essential to clear up one difficulty: that of the technical language used by spiritual, or mystical, theologians at different periods. *Mysticism* is one of the most abused words in all civilized languages, and very many misunderstandings, both in the past and in the present, have been caused by failure to realize that not only do different 'schools' use the same words in varying senses, but that even the 'classical' meaning varies at different periods.

For many people, a poet, an artist, an idealist, even an ideologist, is a 'mystic'. 'Mysticism' may stand for an exaggerated and artificial symbolism, a mania for seeking some occult interpretation of simple, straightforward words; some find a 'mystical' significance in e.g., Communism. In the realm of religion, a fanciful imagination, coupled with certain pious *clichés*, not infrequently suffice to label someone a 'mystic'. There is still a tendency in some circles to draw a sharp differentiating line between the 'great mystics' who, it is implied, held loosely to dogma, and soared aloft above 'institutional religion', and the ordinary, flat-footed rank and file who obediently trudged along, accepting whatever theologians imposed upon them.

Needless to say, the Church knows nothing of all this, and, on account of such misuse of terms the chairs established in certain Catholic universities to teach the subject are commonly known as of 'spiritual', rather than of 'mystical', theology, although the latter term, so long consecrated by use, is still widely employed. *Mystical theology* means directly the experimental knowledge of God enjoyed by contemplative souls and, secondarily, also the theological treatise which studies this contemplation.[1]

This theology is derivative, not primary, and must rest upon a solid foundation of orthodox dogmatic theology. The contemplative life, also, is ascetico-mystical, and although, for obvious reasons, certain forms of religious life are particularly favourable to its development, such are not strictly necessary, and there are, and have been, contemplative saints outside the cloister; indeed, every truly holy life has its contemplative element.

Again, contemplative prayer, even of a high order, is quite distinct from the extraordinary concomitants which may, or may not, accompany it. The 'Transforming union', or 'Spiritual Marriage', lies not in some vision in which the subject receives a wedding ring, but in a union of the will with that of God so perfect that, as says St. John of the Cross, and every mystical saint before him, the two wills have become one; or, to use St. Paul's words: *I live, now not I; but Christ liveth in me.*[2] On the soul's part, there must be fidelity to prayer, and fidelity to the ordinary ascetics of the Christian life. It is for God to do the rest, according as He sees fit. Hence, spiritual theology is concerned with prayer, for the most part, since 'prayer is the spiritual life; it is our reaction to God'.[3]

Mental prayer, in the sense of interior prayer, is prayer in the strictest sense, and must be present in all forms of vocal prayer, even the highest liturgical prayer, on pain of the latter's not being prayer at all. Otherwise, vocal prayer becomes mere 'sounding brass and tinkling cymbal', degenerating into formalism and ritualism, and for those devoid of musical or ceremonial appreciation

---

[1] See *The Spiritual Director, according to the Principles of St. John of the Cross,* by P. Gabriel of St. Mary Magdalen, O. C. D., translated by a Benedictine of Stanbrook Abbey, Mercier Press, Cork, 1952.
[2] Gal. 2:20.
[3] Fr. R. H. J. Steuart, S. J.

the most elaborate choral offices will, sooner or later, mean boredom.

A certain nomenclature and systematization have developed through the centuries, and although there are those who protest against labelling some orderliness, even some technical phraseology, is necessary in mystical as in dogmatic theology. It is no loss to the faithful that the way of prayer has been, to some extent, surveyed, some signposts erected and even an occasional warning notice put up. Nor is it true that such are 'modern'. As we shall see presently, the usual terminology has been in use for a thousand years. It is true that the period immediately preceding the Reformation sees a definite elaboration of 'methods', which would later develop in such wise as to seem, to those brought up under a simpler system, to arrest all initiative; but abuse must not blind us to use, and we find certain stages in the spiritual life clearly distinguished by all the great masters of 'the craft of prayer'.

Turning to the Middle Ages, we find first that the words: 'contemplation', 'prayer' and 'ecstasy'—*contemplatio, oratio, extasis*—were all used in a sense differing from that attached to them today, and to fail to recognize this is to condemn oneself to misunderstand some of the greatest works upon the subject. The first, in particular, was an elastic term, and we must also distinguish between contemplation and contemplative, or mystical, prayer; besides remembering that *oratio mentalis* did not always mean 'mental prayer', as we know it, but often merely vocal prayer 'thought out' without the words being articulated. 'Prayer' usually meant prayer of petition, whether for temporal or spiritual things, but it could include petitions which were very pure and generous. The *Pater noster* came under this head, and so with every petition for God's glory in any connection, or for the soul's own holiness.[4]

---

[4] In the *De Oratione* of Denis the Carthusian, every conceivable request, from the simplest daily needs to the highest spiritual graces for the individual and the Church are included. (*Opera omnia*, t. XLI. S. Maria de Pratis, Tournay, 1912.)

Earlier still, however, *prayer* has also the sense of conversing with God, and this meaning survives into later times and is found in St. Teresa.[5] The monk is bidden to give himself frequently to prayer—*orationi frequenter incumbere*—and anyone who wishes to pray privately—*orare secretius*—is told simply to enter the oratory and do so; those who do not intend to pray just then are to leave the church immediately after the Office, so that those praying shall not be disturbed.[6] Evidently, it was assumed that there would usually be monks there, thus engaged in prayer. Such prayer would certainly be 'mental', at least in the sense just mentioned, which is found in St. Thomas, and probably in the later one, and the same would apply to the 'short' period of private prayer made in common after certain canonical Hours.

In the 'spacious days' of Cluny, it was the accepted custom that the monks remained in church at private prayer after Matins which, always longer in the monastic Breviary than in others, were longer still in Cluniac houses. Yet, when some of the community found it too exhausting to do so, it was lamented as a falling-off from their pristine fervour.[7]

A couple of centuries later, we find the Mendicant Orders doing likewise. We are told that St. Dominic used to spend the time after Matins praying in the church. The celebrated incident in the life of St. Thomas Aquinas, when he was divinely commended and bidden to name a reward for his labours, took place, according to one tradition, when he was praying before Matins in the church of *San Domenico Maggiore* at Naples,[8] and there were other friars there at prayer who testified to the vision.

---

[5] *Life*, c. 8, n. 5.

[6] *Reg. S. Bened.*, cc. 4 and 52.

[7] See *Vie de Saint Hugues de Cluny*, R. P. Dom L'Huillier, O. S. B, Solesmes, 1888.

[8] The voice proceeded not from a crucifix, as usually stated, but from an ancient picture of the crucifixion, painted on wood, which is still shown in the chapel wherein the scene took place.

From the Dominican *Lives of the Brethren*, we learn that to spend the time after the night Office in private prayer, in church or in one's cell, was the usual thing, whilst from St. Bonaventure's directions to his friars, it is plain that among the Franciscans it was usual to pray in their cells after Matins. They are exhorted to do so and given suggestive instructions. Hence, although, except for the Carthusians, who seem to have always had a fixed period assigned in the horarium for private prayer, we do not find a set time assigned to such in monasteries generally, it seems likely that religious put in more private prayer during the twenty-four hours than perhaps some did, or do, in later times. As to how they prayed, we do not really know, save that they used portions of the psalms, doubtless interspersing these with informal prayer of petition, aspirations, and periods of silent adoration; we certainly do know that mystical, and even extraordinary, graces were received in those night hours.

In pre-Reformation times, the different forms of prayer were integrated; there was not the hard-and-fast line between mental, vocal and liturgical prayer often found in modern days. As we have seen, the favourite time for private prayer was just after the Divine Office, when one was already recollected and 'prayerful', and vocal prayer was mingled with mental prayer according to the will of the individual. Great liberty of spirit prevailed, and although we find 'Meditation Books' as early as St. Anselm, who wrote the best known, they laid down no 'points' or arbitrary divisions, but were meant merely as a help, and not a substitute for any grace God might give at the time.

In theory, however, prayer was traditionally divided into Meditation, Prayer and Contemplation, though other words were often used as synonyms, especially in the case of the first. These were parts of one prayer, not states of prayer at different stages of the spiritual life, and they compenetrated on another. They were assigned as proper to beginners, proficients and the perfect respectively, but in practice this seems only to mean that one or other will tend to predominate in the prayer of an individual at different stages of his progress.

Then as now, meditation meant silent reflection upon some incident in the life of Our Lord, or some moral or theological truth. Preceding it, and sometimes replacing it, was what the monastic Orders called *lectio divina*,[9] which meant the prayerful reading of some portion of the Scriptures, with a view not to intellectual but rather to spiritual profit. At a later period in the Middle Ages, this was sometimes called the 'Preparation', and as such is found in the Carmelite method of prayer as drawn up on traditional lines in 1590 by Fr. John of Jesus-Mary (Aravalles), a disciple of St. John of the Cross.

The most difficult word is 'Contemplation', which for centuries remained vague and was used in differing senses. Even the same writer is not always consistent in the meaning he attaches to it, and some, such as St. Bonaventure, never define it at all, although talking much about it. Often they pass from treating of Contemplation as a predominantly intellectual exercise to considering what is really mystical contemplative prayer, without giving any sign of the transition.

Originally, contemplation meant loving knowledge of God. St. Gregory understands it in this sense and calls it a 'grace'. It follows on naturally from 'prayer', in the sense which we have already quoted, since presumably one prays to *know God*, as distinct from knowing *about* Him. In practice, Hugh of St. Victor seems to incline to this view, but in theory he explains the matter differently. Both he and Richard, his brother in religion, seem to hold that contemplation is the rapid grasping as a whole, with a synthetic glance, if one may use more modern language, of the matter formerly worked out in meditation. After a while, one who practises meditation regularly has no need to spend time working out some subject in order

---

[9] Reg. S. Bened., cc. 48 and 49.

to be led on to pray; thanks to practice, aided of course
by grace, he is 'there', so to speak, and can turn easily to
prayer of petition or aspiration as soon as he is on his
knees. Such seems also the opinion of St. Bonaventure.

On the other hand, St. Bernard, and even St. Thomas
Aquinas, equate meditation and contemplation, so that it
is not easy to see any difference. At a later date, Denis
the Carthusian, both a mystic and a scholastic theologian,
says that in *mystical theology*, which for him means infused
contemplation, 'contemplation, meditation and thought
(*cogitatio*) may be said to be one existent thing', and to
him the only difference between meditation and contemplation lies in the subject of thought. In contemplation,
the soul is busied with the Godhead, the Incarnation and
supremely the Blessed Trinity. St. Bonaventure admits
that in practice meditation simply drops out when the
soul reaches the Unitive Way.

With the twelfth century, we find attempts to clarify
the situation. The greatest scholastics were also great
contemplatives, and, in any case, men accustomed to study
in the great schools and later universities, and who were
hammering away at a fixed terminology in the realm of
dogmatic theology, naturally desired something of the
same sort in the case of spiritual theology. After all, misunderstandings must occur where a number of authorities use the same words in different senses; and this is
especially serious, as St. John of the Cross was one day to
emphasize, as a direct result of his experience with souls,
when there is the question of training and guiding others.

Consequently, in this field also the Middle Ages were ages
of development, and we find opposing tendencies, marked
differences of opinion, arguments, criticisms, even mistakes.
At one time there is a tendency to over-elaboration, to be
followed by a reaction in favour of simplicity, and this goes
on until what, historically, we call 'modern times'. Meditation books, such as that of St. Anselm, consisted simply
of short passages of spiritual teaching and prayers, and

he expressly says that those who use them are not to read
more than is necessary to help them to pray. As a son of St.
Benedict, he had been exhorted to *lectio divina,* but neither
for him nor for his brethren, had reading a book ever been
considered an equivalent for praying. The first meditation
books were meant to be merely suggestive. With the rise
of the *devotio moderna,* we have a marked development in
methods, and some are decidedly artificial.

This is to be explained by the spiritual state of the
times. If in recent centuries the tendency has been to
lose the Liturgy, in the fifteenth the danger was the other
way. Offices had become multiplied, till men and women
must often have been honestly worn out by the burden of
choir work. Mental prayer seemed half forgotten in many
a cloister, spiritual life was at a low ebb and had widely
degenerated into formalism and ritualism, when not into
something worse. The Catholic reformers set themselves
to train souls in the interior life, and not only the new
religious foundations but the old Orders also produced
books, both original works and compilations from earlier
authorities, all dealing with mental prayer, in the sense
we now understand it.

Some of the earlier authors had been ahead of their
times, and the success of their books is a proof that these
met a need. In the popular *Scala Claustralium* of Blessed
Guigo the Carthusian (1145) we have the scheme: *lectio
divina,* meditation, prayer, contemplation; but for him the
last named in an experimental union with God which no
meditation can produce, but for which a soul may pray,
since it is no extraordinary grace. The soul is 'athirst',
'aglow with love', and God's answer is contemplation—
obviously the 'infused contemplation' of modern spiritual theology. Since there can be no question of real
'beginners' reaching this stage, we can see how gradually,
as this meaning became attached to contemplation, that
word came to be synonymous with *contemplative or mystical
prayer.* Meditation and contemplation came to mean an

earlier and a later *kind* of prayer, and no longer a mere difference in degree in one kind and the same prayer. Although the latter is a free gift of God, the soul may hope for it, provided that, as we have said already, it is generously resolved to fulfil the 'iron' conditions. In the case of a religious, or a priest, there must also be fidelity to the Rule and practices of his state of life.

Another word which has changed its meaning is *ecstasy*. Certainly up to the age of St. Bonaventure, it is used in two senses. It may suggest the later idea of a state rather implying a weakness, in which the body is so affected that there may be pathological effects, or at least outward signs of something extraordinary, but such is not the usual earlier meaning. For the Victorines, St. Bonaventure and their contemporaries, there is nothing abnormal in that such souls as are serving God very faithfully should sometimes be in *excessu mentis*—the Latin equivalent for extasis.[10] For Richard of St. Victor it is the last stage of prayer before the Transforming union. St. Bonaventure teaches us that all may, and should, pray and strive for it, although like all mystical writers he grants that such a high stage of prayer is rare, at least as a *state;* for God is master of His graces and, for His own purposes, may grant it now and then to a soul at a lower stage. The mystics of the Germano-Flemish school rather incline to the later view. Denis the Carthusian alludes to the body weakening under the assaults of divine love; Tauler cautions his hearers not to desire it or envy those to whom it is granted, since a price must be paid in physical suffering; whilst Ruysbroeck, who places ecstasy at the same point in the spiritual life as does Richard of St. Victor, says it must be resisted, since it weakens the body.[11]

---

[10] *Summa. Theol.*, IIa, IIæ, q. 175, art. 2 and 3; and *De Veritate*, q. 113, art. 2 ad 9.

[11] See the American Dominican Review, *Cross and Crown*, Sept. 1952; *Ruysbroeck*, by H. Graef. The earlier meaning of ecstasy was probably taken from St. Augustine, who says: *It seems to me that all*

Ecstasy, for the mediævals, is simply prayer of infused contemplation which has completely dominated both the will and the understanding: an actuation of the gift of Wisdom, more or less prolonged, wherein the soul enjoys an experimental union with God of a special intensity, through the love which unites it to Him. Such may occur outside of formal 'prayer' time and whilst it lasts the soul is 'ecstatic', that is 'outside itself', or withdrawn from self and absorbed in God. There need not be any extraordinary grace, such as a vision or revelation, and unless the soul be so visited during work, such a state may pass unnoticed. The great Spanish Benedictine abbot García de Cisneros, the reformer of Montserrat, and one of the outstanding spiritual theologians previous to St. John of the Cross, writes: 'Rapture requires not that a man see visions, or indeed aught else, with his bodily eyes, but rather that he be enlightened and enkindled and refreshed, and raised on high through the love he has for his Creator.'[12]

But it is impossible to study the mediæval mystical writers and not feel that at every turn one comes up against a difficulty: there is a link missing between meditation, or 'prayer' in their sense, and contemplation. It is probably to be included in the second, as far as they understood it, but however that be, the fact remains that it is missing. Richard of St. Victor, experienced in dealing with souls, recognizes this, and mentions another kind of contemplation to which we can attain *by our own industry aided by grace*, but he does not treat of it clearly in detail.

St. Anthony of Padua draws a distinction between *mentis elevatio* and *mentis alienatio*. The second is evidently infused contemplation and the first seems that earlier prayer included by St. John under the head 'contemplation', but called by his disciples variously 'acquired', 'active' or 'mixed' contemplation, for reasons which will appear later. In the

---

the saints have been in ecstasy. See *Comm. on the Psalms*, second Discourse on Psalm XXX.

[12] See Peers, *Studies in the Spanish Mystics*, II.

present case it seems intellectual rather than affective. Adam Scot, a thirteenth-century Carthusian (†1213), says the soul prepares itself for the grace of contemplation by practising a lower form of prayer, which seems to be the 'beginners' contemplation' just mentioned. Stephen of Sawley, the Cistercian (†1252), says the soul must go on meditating until it hears the call: *Friend, go up higher*—that is to a more subtle and higher contemplation of the Godhead; but how is the soul to know when this call has really come?[13] It has been suggested that the frontier between the acquired and infused contemplation was crossed 'insensibly', hence the mediævals did not treat of the former.[14] Again, all recognize periods of dryness, or darkness, and some, such as Tauler, distinguish two of these; but such are usually regarded either as a punishment for past sins and unfaithfulness to grace, or at best as periods of spiritual discipline.

None of these explanations meets the difficulty. Infused contemplation, as all agree, is a gift of God, requiring a special actuation of the gifts of the Holy Ghost, especially those of Wisdom and Understanding. Unlike extraordinary graces, it is in the normal way of perfection, and may be desired, prayed for and hoped for, always provided that the soul corresponds with its graces; but one cannot count upon it, 'God alone knoweth why', says St. John of the Cross. Moreover, the difference between it and the earlier contemplation is one of *kind*. The soul is aware that God is acting upon it, whereas in the former state it was aware only of its own gentle activity, which takes the form of 'loving attention' to God, again to cite the Mystical Doctor. There is an action of the Holy Spirit, but it is hidden from the one who prays. From the fact that he is able to remain thus attentive to God, even although

---

[13] *Supplément* to *La Vie Spirituelle*, n. 22, Sept. 1952; *La contemplation au XIIIe siècle*.
[14] See *L'Oraison dans l'Histoire. Cahiers de la Vie Spirituelle* by P. Paul Philippe, O. P., Éditions du Cerf, France.

the prayer may be desperately monotonous—yet withal strangely strengthening and satisfying—he judges that God is working in him, though in a hidden manner. But one who has once known the real, mystical contemplation can never mistake the two, or be 'insensible' to the difference. He may not understand what is happening, but that is another matter.

Finally, few mediæval theologians, save Hugh of Balma and Denis the Carthusian, seem to take much account of psychology. To make a thorough study of the earlier contemplation—whatever one may choose to call it—the missing links, its features and causes, was to be the supreme original contribution to spiritual theology of St. John of the Cross.

I

EARLY SPANISH SPIRITUALITY

T HE GOLDEN AGE OF SPANISH SPIR-
itual theology flowered suddenly, as though a summer were to burst upon us without a springtide.
Not that Spaniards were ignorant of the subject either in
theory or in practice, but previous to the middle of the
fifteenth century they produced scarcely any native ascetical
and mystical writers. Whereas in former days they could
boast an Isidore, a Leander and lesser lights, the mediæval
period proper was one of importation and imitation. Works
of foreign writers were translated and for spiritual, as well
as for dogmatic theology, Spain was long content to draw
upon the common heritage of Western Christendom. Then,
roughly about the second quarter of the fifteenth century,
there begins a long line of native writers who have assimilated the masterpieces of other lands and are becoming
increasingly original, until we reach the Midsummer with
St. John of the Cross and St. Teresa the Great.

But just because they are themselves, not only are the
'giants' apt to overshadow, almost to eclipse, predecessors
whose work well repays study, but the impression is easily
gained that not only was each an outstanding genius—as
was, of course, the case—but that they were more or less
entirely independent investigators, owing little or nothing
to those who had gone before them. Such is not the case.
One of the leading authorities on St. John[1] has written
that the saint owed much to his predecessors, even though
his own contribution to mystical theology was to be so
outstanding as one day to win him the title of a Doctor
of the Universal Church.

---

[1] P. Gabriele di Santa Maria Maddalena, O. C. D., *San Giovanni della
Croce, Direttore spirituale*, Florence, 1942, translated by a Benedictine
of Stanbrook Abbey, Mercier, Cork, 1952.

The present study attempts to answer two questions: to whom was he chiefly indebted and to what extent? For reasons which will appear as we go on, it seems possible to treat the subject under three heads: the Victorines, St. Bonaventure and the writers of the Germano-Flemish school. We must begin, however, with a short general survey of pre-fifteenth-century Spanish spirituality, and we must end by considering the saint in his own historical setting.

Mediæval Spain produced no writers of the calibre of the Victorines, no 'school' such as that of the Rhineland and the Low Countries, and when eventually we do have native Spanish writers, their works are ascetical. An explanation frequently offered is that the Spanish outlook was too practical to be mystical; but although a practically minded people, then as now, they could reconcile that characteristic with high mystical life. We need only read the Letters of St. Teresa to prove that, and though we have so few left of the many we know St. John wrote, those few suffice to show that the *Doctor Mysticus* could come down to earth when obedience required. Business letters of his are short, clear, 'business-like', and it was 'God's goldfinch', as Anne of Jesus called him, and not Teresa, who wrote, about a certain legal document which a superior had neglected to have properly signed and sealed: 'I have greatly regretted that the contract with the Fathers of the Company has not been drawn up; because as I see them, they are not people who keep their word.... Note then, that I advise you ... to discuss with Señor Gonzalo Muñoz the purchase of that other house ... and that the deeds be drawn up.... Tell few people about this and do it; as sometimes one ruse cannot be foiled except by another.'[2]

The intense fervour of Spanish faith was a byword and, after all, faith is the absolutely indispensable foundation of all spiritual life! The same faith which sent Spaniards into

---

[2] *Letter IV,* to Mother Anne of St. Albert, Prioress of Caravaca.

the fighting line, to their battle-cry of *Sant Iago y serra!*[3]
to die fighting, as simply the natural duty of a Christian
and patriot, sent other Spaniards into the many religious
houses they raised in order that there might always be
those to adore, praise and intercede, on the 'mountain',
for those struggling in the plain. It is unthinkable that
He who, as John reminds us, is ever seeking souls far
more earnestly than the souls are seeking Him, did not
grant triumphs in the spiritual field fully comparable
to that of Las Navas de Tolosa in the material one. The
thanksgiving for that victory over the infidel took the
form of the great Cistercian abbey of Las Huelgas,[4] at
Burgos, where they enclosed one hundred contemplative
nuns as spiritual reinforcements, so that the long vista
of its tremendous choir still takes one's breath away. The
Carthusian Order, contemplative by excellence, made many
and magnificent foundations in Spain, so there seems to
have been a sufficiency of vocations to such a life. Seemingly we must seek further, and perhaps their exceptional
political circumstances may suggest a reason for the lack
of mystical writings. Of mediæval Spain may be said, with
special emphasis, what has been said of mediæval Europe
as a whole: it was a camp with a church in the background.
The Spaniard had the Moslem literally at his gates. Spain
sent no great crusading armies to Palestine but she waged
a perpetual crusade at home. For centuries, more than half
the country was in the hands of the Moslem and had to
be won back piecemeal. Freedom as well as faith was at
stake. The situation bred a type of mind that was realist
and simple; incidentally excellent soil in which to plant
the seeds of an intense spiritual life, but less favourable
to the growth of speculative studies. The atmosphere of
wartime is not favourable to writing except of a certain
kind, and that kind is not mystical theology. Anxieties

---

[3] 'St. James and close the ranks!'
[4] Founded in 1212, by Alfonso VIII of Castile and his wife, Eleanor
Plantagenet, daughter of Henry II of England.

and preoccupations cannot be kept out of even a cloister, nor is it altogether desirable that they should, since there must be no selfish escapism from the trials our brethren are facing; only at such a time one is not at one's best for writing theological treatises. Other more peaceful lands had produced what was needed, and the common tongue of Western Christendom rendered such works accessible to such as were likely to read them.

Again, the peculiar conditions had another effect upon the Church in Spain. Side by side with the religious houses of the old Orders, three Spanish military Orders of importance were founded, not to mention a number of lesser ones which were eventually absorbed in the former;[5] and when the mendicants appeared in Spain two such Orders, the Mercedarians and Trinitarians, had as their special work the ransoming of, and caring for, Christian captives taken by the Moors. Thus spiritual energy was directed into a new channel, and a very active one.

But there was another factor which probably militated against original writing on certain aspects of the spiritual life. The peculiar religious situation in Spain directly affected the attitude of theologians towards mystical theology, and this persisted up to the time of St. Teresa. The rival Moslem power had a religious tradition, and was culturally superior to Christian Spain for many a day. Islam produced not only masterpieces of craftmanship and architecture, mathematical studies which outshone those of its Christian opponents, but also a philosophy and pseudo-mysticism which had a very real appeal. Just as, thanks to the works of the Moslem philosophers, Averroés and Avicenna,[6] Aristotle would remain suspect at the schools

---

[5] The Order of Calatrava, founded in Castile in the twelfth century under Cistercian influence; the Order of Sant Iago de Compostela, also in the twelfth century; that of Alcantara in 1119, and that of *Our Lady of Ransom*, under the influence of the friars of the same name, in 1218.

[6] Averroés was born at Cordova in 1128 and died in Morocco in 1198. Despite his heterodoxy, there was much in his work which was

of Paris and elsewhere until the Angel of the Schools
would make of his philosophy, as has been said, 'the four-
square walls of the City of God', so also the Alumbrados,
or Spanish Illuminists, with their extravagances, led to a
deep distrust of any sort of spirituality which might seem
to diverge from the plain, familiar, highway walked by
the plain man, be he churchman or layman. Even in the
later days of the Catholic Kings, Ferdinand and Isabella,
and their immediate successors, quite as many people fell
foul of the Inquisition owing to false mysticism as to false
doctrine, and heresy and Illuminism were convertible terms.
The fear of either led, as was only to be expected, to panic
and extremes, so that even a Teresa of Jesus might become
suspect and a Grand Inquisitor might condemn a good
vernacular Bible, and many a sound spiritual work, in his
wholesale onslaught on dangerous books; whilst parents
anxious for their children's spiritual welfare were refusing
to have them taught to read, so as to insure them against
the danger of Illuminist literature.[7]

---

very able, and St. Thomas does him full justice, even whilst pointing
out his errors. It is curious that the mediæval scholar who knew most
about him was the English Carmelite, John Baconthorpe, although
he remained perfectly orthodox. Born about 1290, at Baconthorpe
in Norfolk, he entered the Carmelite house at Blakeney in the same
county, and studied at Oxford and Paris, where he took his doctorate
and subsequently taught, being Regent of Studies in the Paris house
of his Order. Later, he returned to England, taught at Cambridge
and again at Oxford, eventually becoming Provincial of England. He
died about 1348. He belonged to no 'school' and has been called a
mixture of Nominalist and Realist. The Occamists borrowed from
him, as did the Englishman, Thomas Bradwardine of Canterbury.
(See *Ephemerides Carmelitice*, Nov. 1948. Libreria fiorentina, Firenze.
Article by Fr. Nilo di S. Brocardo, O. C. D.).

Avicenna, whom St. Thomas seems to have preferred on certain
grounds, was born at Bokara in 980, dying in Persia in 1037.
[7] Sister Catherine of Christ (de Balmaseda) was an example. She
entered the Carmel of Medina del Campo in 1571, was taught to
read and write, and became Prioress of Soria and later of Pamplona
and Barcelona, dying in 1594. She was an exemplary and capable
religious. (Letters of St. Teresa, Vol. IV, p. 186, Edn. of the Benedictines of Stanbrook, Baker.)

But all this does not mean that Spaniards were not thinkers and students. The early Christian period was much influenced by the *Organum* of Aristotle, which had been translated with a commentary by St. Isidore of Seville; and this influence persisted, although Plato was also greatly appreciated. Later on, spiritual writers who were Platonic and Augustinian were more in evidence than those who were Aristotelian and Thomist. But perhaps the most remarkable influence was that of Seneca, himself a native of Cordova. Even although Christianity rejected his pessimism, the Stoic teaching as to dominion of the passions, frugality and simplicity—albeit the philosopher did not always practise what he taught—prepared the way for the later ascetic and mystical writers. Seneca suited the Spanish inclination to the moral and practical rather than to the metaphysical. On the fifteenth century, his works were to be found in the library catalogues of royal, aristocratic and clerical personages, not only in Spain but in the Spanish Netherlands.[8] In 1529, Erasmus published the first critical edition of Seneca, and we find him quoted constantly. Even St. John of the Cross bears traces of him, and the Franciscan mystic, Fray Francisco of Osuna, whose works so helped St. Teresa, cites him repeatedly.[9] And further, when that same Teresa chose a soubriquet for John of the Cross, her 'half-Friar', she called him her 'Little Seneca'—*Senequito*—and sometimes 'Seneca', *tout court*!

Turning to Christian sources, in the Peninsula, as everywhere else, Holy Scripture came first and foremost; then came the Fathers and then Pseudo-Denys. As every reader of St. John of the Cross can testify, his works are saturated with Scripture, and how assiduously he studied the Bible we can learn from contemporary evidence. Those

---

[8] Such as the celebrated scholar Justus Lipsius of Brussels, the secretary of Cardinal Granvella.
[9] See the *Third Spiritual Alphabet*, Treatise 21, translated by a Benedictine of Stanbrook Abbey, Burns & Oates, London.

who lived with him stated that the only book he kept in his cell was a Bible. *The Institution of the first Monks*—really the primitive Carmelite Rule—prescribed for the reading of all, and for special study in the noviciate, is full of scripture. John of Jesus-Mary (Aravalles), one of those trained in the first noviciate at Pastrana, of which John was a novice-master, tells us that the saint's knowledge of the Scriptures was such that he, the witness, and his fellow religious believed that it was infused. Be that as it may, the Carmelite Superiors prescribed a daily Scripture lecture in their houses of studies, and such was the rule at Salamanca University.

Even apart from this, Spaniards were great Bible readers. There as elsewhere, those who were able used Latin Bibles, but in 1252 Alfonso X ordered a vernacular translation to be made, which seems to have remained in general use and sufficed until 1524, when a new version of the Epistles was published at Alcalá, to be followed later by the Gospels. In 1553, there appeared a complete new translation of the Bible, and there were several Spanish versions of the Psalms. Such were published in 1529, 1538, 1550 and 1555, and in 1550 other books of the Old Testament were also translated into Spanish. There were also separate vernacular versions of the Penitential and Gradual Psalms.

Then came a change. Yet another Spanish version of the Bible had published at Antwerp in 1543, but was forbidden shortly afterwards, and in 1551, Juan de Valdés, the Grand Inquisitor, forbade vernacular versions altogether. Yet even so, there was no objection raised to even long passages of the Bible being cited in other Spanish books, and it is thought that Spanish contemporary writers deliberately quoted, and that at length, in order thus to supply to their readers in some measure for what the new Index denied them. Not that such is the only explanation of the lavish use of Scripture extracts. Luis de Granada constantly quoted from Scripture, Osuna and John of Avila exhort their readers to read the Spanish Bibles, and look up the passages to which they refer them. As for St. John of the Cross, although he wrote for a limited circle, namely the Carmelite nuns of the Reform, and for one devout laywoman, Ana de Peñalosa, a widow of Segovia and a great friend of the Order, for whom he wrote the *Living Flame of Love*, he assumes that all are familiar with Old and New Testaments. And, be it remembered, only a minority—probably a small one, to judge from St. Teresa's rebuke to Mother Mary of St. Joseph, the former María de Salazar, related to the great house of Cerda—knew Latin well enough to read the Vulgate easily.[10] True, the saint constantly uses quotations in an 'accommodated' sense, as do the Fathers, most mediæval theologians and many modern preachers; but if now and then his interpretations seem farfetched, they are never extravagant as are many Patristic ones, such as some of St. Gregory. John is not a writer who 'can make anything mean anything'.

The discipline in this matter of vernacular Bible reading was more severe in Spain than elsewhere, even in Italy; and although they obeyed not all orthodox Spanish theologians agreed with it. New editions of the Index added a number of vernacular spiritual works, originals or translations, to the list of prohibited books, and readers of St. Teresa will remember how she felt the deprivation. Her allusions to 'the Lutherans' have been somewhat airily dismissed by a recent writer as a generic term of disapproval, on a par with 'Fascist' in our day, and it is implied that Lutheranism was non-existent in Spain. This is simply incorrect. Genuine Lutheranism had affected some spiritual writers and, as a matter of course, false mysticism followed on the heels of false doctrine. A namesake of the Grand Inquisitor, Juan de Valdés, published an *Alfabeto cristiano*, commentaries on St. Paul, and a work entitled *Ciento y Diez consideraciones divinis*,[11] all in or about 1550,

---

[10] See *Letters of St. Teresa*, vol. II, n. 141 (Baker, London); also, Vilnet, *Bible et S. Jean de la Croix* (Desclée).
[11] *A hundred and ten considerations upon divine things.*

wherein he teaches Justification by faith alone—Luther's basic doctrine—personal interpretation of Scripture, and definitely Arian and anti-Trinitarian opinions of his own. Nor is his work free from Illuminism, for he teaches that, by an interior enlightening, God causes us to be certain of our salvation, and that anyone who receives this must renounce the light of human reason and the exercise of his will. Thus Valdés begins with Lutheranism, although he ceases to be a follower of Luther and never becomes a Calvinist.[12]

The old Priscillianist heresy also lifted its head again, and other writers wrested to their destruction the writings of that universally used authority, Pseudo-Denys, the 'Areopagite'. Time, ink and acrimony have been expended upon the fifth-century Syrian author, who, by adopting his curious style, whereby he makes himself appear as St. Paul's Athenian convert, caused his works to be accepted as scarcely less authoritative than the Bible. Whether he did this with the intention of deceiving his readers, as has been held by some scholars, or whether he was trying to conciliate orthodox and heretics, as others have suggested, will probably never be known.

He seems to have been a Neo-Platonist, and is first mentioned in the middle of the sixth century at a conference between Catholics and moderate Monophysites at Constantinople. In 827, a copy of his works was presented to Louis the Pious, and Scotus Eriugena made a Latin translation for Charles the Bald. It seems impossible to doubt the personal piety of the writer, who may or may not have been named *Denys*, but it has been suggested

---

[12] The incident of St. Teresa's rejection of the would-be postulant, who announced that she would bring her Bible with her to Carmel, may take on rather a different aspect in the light of the new situation created by the Index. Certainly, if the said Bible was in Spanish, trouble might have ensued. Had any suspicion of disobedience to lawful authority fallen upon the new Carmelite foundations, it would have been fatal to the Reform, which did not lack enemies.

that his style was a dramatic 'conceit', sufficiently familiar
to his contemporaries not to cause misunderstanding.[13]
Certainly the fact must be faced that every spiritual writer,
from the Victorines to St. John of the Cross, follows him,
more or less, even St. Thomas drawing upon him when he
thinks fit so to do. We trace his influence in the English
mystical work, the Cloud of Unknowing, one of the clearest
anticipations there is of St. John's teaching, and French-
men, Dutch, Flemings, Germans, Italians and Spaniards,
all make use of this 'mystery man' who has been hailed
diversely as a saint and an impostor. Although it is highly
likely that it was because they believed him to be St. Paul's
disciple that mediæval theologians felt bound to follow
him, even whilst using him they improved upon him; and
he furnished them with a convenient phraseology when
it came to systematizing their spiritual theology, as much
as did Aristotle in the case of their dogmatic studies. But
such Dionysian expressions as 'annihilation', for example, often used in a recognized and quite orthodox sense,
underwent a change, and we find not only a Neo-Platonist
but an oriental and Gnostic philosophy and mysticism
causing anxiety in Spain, not only to the Inquisition but
to all earnest clergy and faithful. Alumbrados taught that
a soul could be buried in an infinite essence, wherein it
loses personality and is in a state of perfection in which
it is no longer responsible for its sins. From this it was
a short step to vulgar imposture, and the emergence of
such pseudo-mystical frauds as the notorious Magdalena
de la Cruz and the cases which from time to time were
brought to St. John of the Cross.

Returning to the latter, we are told again by John
of Jesus-Mary that the saint often used Denys and the

---

[13] See *Patrology*, Otto Bardenhewer (Herder, 1908), pp. 535–577. Also,
Les Pères Apostoliques et leur époque, by Mgr. Freppel (Paris, 1870) for
the dramatic element in early Christian writings, and Saudreau,
La Vie de l' Union à Dieu. Also *A History of Philosophy*, Copleston, Vol.
II (Burns & Oates, London, 1950).

writings of the saints, which means firstly those of the
Fathers; but it is not easy to fasten upon every allusion
to earlier writers. Unlike his contemporaries in Spain
and elsewhere, John never gives us a string of quotations,
except in the case of Holy Scripture. Nor with the exception of a few Patristic passages, all from the Breviary, does
he even mention authors by name, with the exception of
Pseudo-Denys and St. Thomas. He works the authorities
into his own text and makes them his own. Consequently,
we have to trace his borrowings from earlier writers rather
laboriously. Probably, the reason was that he wrote, as he
said, for 'certain persons of the Reformed Carmel' and
not for the general public, at least in the first place. His
object was practical and he saw no need of giving his
readers chapter and verse for everything he said. The
Office rendered them reasonably familiar with the names
and, often, the titles of the Patristic works cited, and
moreover, he gave the community for which he wrote
specially frequent spiritual conferences, and instructed
them, in public and in private according to their needs.
Another reason, however, is undoubtedly, that he had so
completely assimilated the works of his predecessors that
the statement, the simile, the exhortation, was there at
hand as he needed it, and without stating where it was
to be found he simply wove it into his own work. Again,
he is at once original and traditional, and certain figures
of speech and expressions had long become the common
property of all spiritual theologians. We find the same
language century after century; all the later writers draw
upon the earlier authorities, and as says his most able
modern editor: 'We have not read St. John of the Cross
long before we find ourselves in the full current of mystical
tradition', and again: 'St. John of the Cross read widely in
mediæval mystical theology, and assimilated a great part
of what he read'.[14] What he did do was to clear away

---

[14] See the General Introduction by P. Silverio de Santa Teresa (now
General of the Discalced Carmelites) to his edition of the Works

the long, often contradictory digressions and repetitions of the mediævalists, separate the essential from the non-essential, and in short do for mystical theology much of what St. Thomas Aquinas did for the subject in general.

Having sketched in lightly the earlier Spanish background, we can now consider those to whom he seems to have owed most. These are the Victorines, St. Bonaventure and the Germano-Flemish school. His Spanish contemporaries and their immediate predecessors can be treated more conveniently when we come to assess his own distinctive contribution.

---

of St. John of the Cross. (Translated by the late Prof. E. A. Peers, Burns Oates, London, 1934; revised edition 1953.)

II

THE VICTORINES

I. HUGH OF ST. VICTOR

THE INFLUENCE OF THE VICTORINES upon later theologians was so great that one despairs of doing it justice. Of St. Bonaventure it has been said that 'he followed and completed their teaching'. His monumental works are full of lengthy quotations from them; not a spiritual writer of Western Christendom but seems to have been indebted to them in some degree. St. Thomas quotes from them and accepts their definitions with, at most, only slight modifications. Denis the Carthusian, 'the last of the Scholastics', does likewise, and so it is down the years, until we come to the fifteenth-century Spaniards and St. John of the Cross.

When we speak of 'the Victorines', we mean really Hugh and Richard, although the famous house of Augustinians produced also Adam, who has his high place as a hymn writer who was also a poet; Andrew, the Biblical commentator and Hebraist, some of whose interpretations can be rather startling, and make us realize that, after all, the ecclesiastical authorities of the Ages of Faith could be remarkably tolerant;[1] and Odo, whose few letters suffice to show that he must have led an interior life quite in the spirit of his abbey.

Hugh, who has been called a 'second Augustine', was born in 1096 or 1097, probably at Hammersleben, near Halberstadt, in Saxony, where he was certainly brought up, or possibly at Ypres, and seems to have belonged to the

---

[1] He became Prior and, in 1174, with two other Canons, was sent to found the abbey of Wigmore, in Herefordshire, of which he became Abbot. (See Dugdale, Monasticon, vol. VI, pp. 444-448. Also, *The Study of the Bible in the Middle Ages*, by Beryl Smalley, Oxford, Clarendon Press, 1941.)

family of the counts of Blankenberg in the Harz region.
He entered the house of Augustinian Canons in his home
town, but either—as has been suggested—on account
of political disorders, or because his family opposed his
vocation, in 1115 he transferred to St. Victor's at Paris,
founded some years previously by the celebrated scholar,
William of Champeaux. In 1133, he became Prior, and
died in 1141. He was both a philosopher and theologian and, for his day, something of a scientist. Among
his works is a Bestiary, and although, even in the two
former subjects, his views can be called in question at
times, such is the fate of most pioneers, and he performed a great work in synthesizing and systematizing
the teachings of the Fathers, and so helping to lay the
foundations of the mighty edifice of the Church's formal
theology. As regards his mystical teaching we may quote
the words of a leading Spanish authority: 'The school
of St. Victor studies the state of the soul in its different
stages of ascent to God with great delicacy, as regards
psychological analysis'.[2] The same disciple of St. John
of the Cross, John of Jesus-Mary, to whom we owe so
many interesting details about his master, speaks in high
terms of Hugh, whom he had evidently read as a young
friar, and when the works of the saint were attacked by
the Inquisition after his death, the brilliant Augustinian,
Fray Basilio Ponce de León,[3] used the Victorines, among
others whom we shall meet soon, as a standard whereby
to judge the censured propositions.

With Hugh we have a certain classification of the stages
of the interior life, and he uses a phraseology which later
writers would sometimes clarify but never completely
change. Nothing could be further from the truth than
the statement, not infrequently heard, that all system and

---

[2] *Introducción a la Historia de la Mística en España* by Doct. Pedro Sáinz
Rodriquez. (Editorial Voluntad, Madrid, 1927.)
[3] He was nephew to the famous spiritual writer, Luis de León.
His defence of St. John of the Cross was so successful that it put
an end to the case against the saint.

technical language in connection with the life of prayer came in only with Tridentine days, thereby spoiling the earlier simplicity!

It is impossible to fix the dates of Hugh's works and we find much overlapping when we come to study his teaching on prayer. Clearly, he is groping after words which will make his teaching easier for beginners, for we know that he was a novice master, and he seems to use expressions tentatively and with varying shades of meaning in different books. When he comes to treat of the higher stages of the spiritual life, he experiences the usual impossibility of expressing the inexpressible. *Expertus potest dicere!* Obviously, he does speak from experience, and his language is often very beautiful, but as to explaining what he knows to those who have not known it—tongue and pen alike fail.

There is an exaggerated idealism about his teaching, and later on St. Thomas would reduce it to better defined and clearer concepts. He also holds that the soul is the true man, and the body only an organ of the soul, not an essential part of the human composite. The least satisfactory portion of his teaching, for the present purposes, however, concerns that important period of the spiritual pilgrimage known as the Illuminative Way: the stage of 'Progressives', who have passed the beginners' stage but are yet far from perfection and need help. St. John's greatest contribution to the subject would be precisely here.

Hugh's most frequently quoted works are the *De Arrha Animæ* (i.e., the earnest, or pledge, of love in the shape of the bridal gift given to a bride in former times, as the later engagement ring); the *De Anima*, the *De laude caritatis*, a devotional work, the *Eruditionis didascalicæ*, the *De institutione novitorum* and the first of his nineteen *Homilies* on Ecclesiastes. Of these eighteen are an exposition of the Book, verse by verse, ascetic not mystical, and rather recalling the style of some patristic commentaries; but the first is a valuable and beautiful treatise from which later writers, including both St. Thomas and St. Bonaventure, cite passages verbatim. From it comes the well-known simile of the fire and the log, used by so many mystical writers including St. John of the Cross.[4]

In this Homily, we read:

> There are three ways of considering spiritual things: by thought, by meditation, and by contemplation. It is a simple thought when the mind is struck by an idea which, without having been sought, offers itself by means of the senses or the memory; and at which it does not stop. There is meditation when the mind lingers at something, turns it over, and by assiduous consideration tries to explain it, or by searching to penetrate what is hidden. But if the mind wills by a penetrating gaze to embrace at the same time divers matters it should consider, then there is contemplation. Between meditation and contemplation there is this difference: meditation is always concerned with matters hidden from our understanding, but contemplation with matters that are already made manifest, either according to their nature or according to our capacity.[5]

In other words, contemplation grasps the subject in a synthetic 'gazing' without needing to analyse it. 'In meditation there is question of one thing; in contemplation of many things or even everything.' We have here the 'confused knowledge' of St. John and other mystics, and St. Bonaventure similarly describes these stages of prayer. Hugh reminds us that study and reflection will not carry us far unless there be also holiness of life: 'Purity of intention, prayer and alms'. For him, as for John, the way of Christian perfection is *ascetico-mystical*.

Meditation on the vanity of this world is proper to the 'imperfect'; to the 'perfect' belongs the 'contemplation of God'. There follows the simile of the green log in the fire.

---

[4] *Dark Night*, c. X; Ascent, B. I, cc. 5 and 11; B. II, c. 8.
[5] Hugo S. Vict., Hom. in Eccles., vol. 1; P. L., CLXXV.

At first the fire seizes upon the wood with difficulty but when, fanned by a stronger draught, it begins to burn up the latter, dark smoke belches forth in clouds, so that the flames are hardly seen. Then, little by little, all the damp is dried out, the smoke and steam disappear, and only the bright, glowing fire can be discerned. Nor does the conquering flame rest until it has drawn the whole into itself; the log has passed into the likeness of the fire. All crackling and noise dies down, for now there is no diversity between the fire and the wood, and all is silence.

Hugh says that the human heart is like that.

The flame is some spark of divine fire or love, which attacks the evil desires and disturbs the passions, which put up some resistance. Then the mind is strengthened by the flame of love, and urged on to the contemplation of truth. Finally, by assiduous contemplation the heart will be penetrated by all affection, and in that selfsame sweetness, as wholly aglow and turned into the fire of love, freed from all noise and disturbance, it rests most peacefully.... The soul asks only to be plunged back alone into the fire of love, in deepest peace and happiness. Then, with its whole heart turned into the fire of love, it feels that God is truly all in all; since He is received with such intimate love that beside Him nothing is left, even of the heart itself.

We see here the double current of contemplation, which is brought out more clearly by Bonaventure and Denis the Carthusian. The distinction is often drawn between 'Cherubic' and 'Seraphic', or between 'Intellectual' and 'Sapiential' contemplation. In the former the gift of Understanding predominates, in the latter that of Wisdom, and, as we are in this world, the former must end in the latter. St. Thomas teaches us that contemplation is 'the simple act of gazing on the truth', and though essentially in the

intellect it terminates in an act of the will.[6] Practically
speaking, in the cases of the great mystical saints the line
cannot be drawn. St. Thomas has been classed as 'Cherubic', as has St. John of the Cross; whilst St. Bonaventure
is the 'Seraphic' Doctor. But all were great thinkers and
great ecstatics, and comparisons between them as regards
their union with God seem not only odious but futile!

St. John of the Cross inserts this simile of the log when
he is about to treat of the *Dark Night* of the soul, which
is to prepare it for perfect union with God.[7] We have
the same resistance of the 'log' as the 'night' envelops it,
the same sufferings. But although both writers meet at
the end of the road, Hugh has leapt from the stage of
meditation to that of infused or 'mystical' contemplation,
even seemingly to that of the prayer of Union, and he
has telescoped the two 'nights': that of the senses and
that of the spirit. St. John's soul is emerging from the
meditation of the Purgative Way, and is entering upon the
Illuminative Way. Its prayer is changing and at first the
change is disconcerting, for the new 'acquired' or 'active'
contemplation—what St. John himself calls the prayer
of 'loving attention'—is not sensibly consoled, and may
be desperately monotonous in its aridity. Moreover, as
the Mystical Doctor explains in very unequivocal terms,
the said soul is very far from perfection. Although for
Hugh the divine love is carrying out the same process of
burning out imperfections as for John, the soul might
simply be discouraged and bewildered unless aided from
some other source. We are a long way from the clarity
and skilled guidance of the Carmelite.

Nevertheless, there is no mistaking the influence of the
earlier theologian. John must have read his descriptions
of the later stage with delight, as being that of a kindred
spirit. 'In this same way... this divine fire of contemplative
love... before it unites and transforms the soul into itself,

---

[6] *Summa Theol.*, IIa, IIæ, q. 180, art. 1.
[7] *Dark Night*, c. X.

first purges it of all its contrary accidents. By this dark
night of contemplation, these humours become visible to
the soul because it is so brightly illumined....' The fire
which transforms it, that is to say, 'the very light and the
loving wisdom, are the same that in the beginning purge
and prepare it'.[8] This 'dark contemplation' causes the soul
to realize its poverty and wretchedness, 'although it is no
worse than before either in itself or in relation to God'.[9]

Evidently, Hugh is not satisfied, for he presently intro-
duces a form of prayer between meditation and contemplation called *speculatio*.[10] He now tells us that in meditation
there is 'anxiety'—*sollicitudo*, in *speculatio* there is *admiratio*—a certain reverential wonder or awe, which includes
the English 'admiration' but adds something to it; and in
contemplation there is sweetness. We shall meet this word
again in St. Bonaventure, but the latter calls it an intellectual contuition: that is an apprehension of God in an
effect perceived under the influence of the gift of Understanding. It is a form of prayer tending to quietude, but it
is not passive at first, but exercised by discursive thinking
and investigation. It does not carry us much further but
suggests the 'beginners' contemplation', later to be known
as 'Acquired Contemplation' by Carmelite theologians.

In a short essay: *De meditando*,[11] Hugh explains, for the
only time, in some detail what he means by meditation;
and it is easy to see that everyone who has ever produced
a typical 'meditation book' has, knowingly or unknowingly,
borrowed from him. In meditation, we think over the manner, cause and reason of whatever we are investigating: what
is it? how is it? why is it? We may choose our subject from
created things, morals, or the Scriptures, but still there is

---

[8] *Dark Night*, B. II, c. 10.
[9] *Ibid.*
[10] St. Thomas equates *Speculatio* with meditation. The word means
'beholding', as in a mirror, and means also, therefore, to see a cause
in its effect, wherein its likeness is reflected. See *Summa Theol.*, IIa,
IIæ, q. 180, art. 3.
[11] Hugo S. Vict., *P. L.*, CLXXVI.

no consideration of the people who simply cannot practise this discursive meditation. Nor is there any warning for the unfortunates for whom one day the heavens fall, and they find they cannot do it any longer, although there is no sign of the high prayer that Hugh and his contemporaries imply should follow. The 'anxiety' of meditation refers to the attention and effort of the soul which, although of course aided by grace, has plenty of work to do at this stage. He warns that, should it relax, it will lose all the ground previously gained. As for the *admiratio*, it is now used in a sense very frequent in the Middle Ages, especially after the appearance of the Franciscans; namely the wonder with which a man gazes upon, or even considers mentally, the material creation: the beauty of earth, the marvels of the heavens and of nature generally. The same effect can be produced by beautiful music. Under the impression, the beholder may break into ejaculatory prayer, and the Psalms are expressly instanced as providing such aspirations of praise and thanksgiving, and adoration. Of course St. Francis' *Canticle of the Sun* is such an outstanding example, and Hugh himself tells us: 'Heaven and earth, and all that is therein cease not to tell me to love my God'.[12] St. John of the Cross, poet and nature lover, who used to take his novices out to the lonely countryside and then bid them disperse and pray; who sings of the hills, the forest, the meadow-land spangled with blossoms, the wooded valleys and the streams, is another example; but although such admiration can lead to intense prayer this can only be provided the subject does not rest in the natural beauty, but rises forthwith from nature to the Creator. In the latter case, we have the contemplation which St. Thomas says is: a simple act of gazing upon the truth,[13] and one far advanced in the spiritual life may be even thrown into that contemplation which is 'a foretaste of Beatitude'.[14] Nevertheless, an artist, a poet, a musician can

---

[12] *De Anima*, col. 131; P. L., CLXXVII.
[13] *Summa Theol.*, IIa, IIæ, q. 180, art. 7 and 3.
[14] *Ibid.*, art. 4.

be entranced or enraptured by the same sights or sounds, but without rising to God at all. In itself, such 'admiration' is certainly not mystical and need not be even religious. It may, however, prepare a soul in right dispositions for that special co-operating grace which will bear it far beyond and above the loveliest natural sights earth can show, until it catches a glimpse of Absolute Beauty, and 'needs must love the highest when it sees it'. Only in practice we must be on our guard, for it is just through stopping at nature alone that so many people have come to abuse the word 'mysticism'.[15]

It must be remembered, moreover, that although for the sake of clarity certain kinds of prayer are linked to certain phases of the spiritual life, there are no hard and fast rules, or fixed frontiers. Not only in practice do those phases shade off gradually, but many a soul seems for years to be drifting between two of the fixed points. Again, God is absolute master of His gifts. He can and does grant high mystical graces sporadically, sometimes even to a soul which seems at too low a level for such, if He so will and so bless! Every mystical writer tends to speak from his or her own experience, and those who come earlier have less experience of others whereby to amplify their own. Hence the inconclusive nature of much in Hugh of St. Victor.

In his *De institutione Novitiorum*, a most practical work on the training of novices, and containing all the traditional teaching given to them in all periods and all institutes, he prescribes *lectio divina*, wherein they are to ponder over the Scriptures, which arouse love of God and contempt of the world. He seems to be borrowing from the well-known work, the *Scala Claustralium*, once, like so much, ascribed

---

[15] A striking modern instance is recorded in the life of Cardinal Merry del Val. In August 1921 he was in the Dolomites and set out very early one morning to ascend the Cima Boé (over 10,000 ft.) with his secretary, the present Cardinal Canali, and a guide. They reached the summit at noon, and gazing upon the towering mountains, bathed in a glory of sunshine, amid absolute silence, the Cardinal burst into the Gloria in Excelsis, and sang it through to the end (*Il Cardinale Merry del Val*, Pio Cenci, p. 503, Rome, 1933.)

to St. Bernard, but now known to be the work of Guigo
de Chastel, General of the Carthusians, who was almost a
contemporary, being born in 1083 and dying in the odour
of sanctity in 1137. This 'ladder' of prayer has four rungs:
reading, meditation, prayer and contemplation; the first is
from Scripture, and in the second the mind searches out
the hidden truth therein. Then the monk turns to God and
prays for grace to amend all that is amiss in his life, and
embrace all that is good. In contemplation, the mind is
uplifted to God, whilst it 'savours the joys of eternal sweetness'. At this stage, all earthly things are forgotten, and
this state is the work of the Holy Spirit. This Carthusian
work has an alternative title: *De modo orandi*, and in those
centuries, when nobody dreamed of claiming literary rights,
Hugh adopted the same title for another book of his own.[16]
There again, he treats the earlier stages of prayer, but goes
further, and, as always, as he rises higher he becomes clearer
in his explanations. He follows the same line as in his book
for novices, and inserts the 'Reading' though without nam-
ing it. He advises his readers to prepare themselves, before
their formal prayer time, by devout considerations, such
as their spiritual poverty, the mercy of God, the shortness
of life, etc. Thus they will not come to prayer unprepared
or lukewarm. They should then pray for grace and stir up
compunction, which will drive away sloth and prepare the
way for *devotion*, which means not merely sensible devotion, but chiefly that will to betake oneself to the things
which belong to the service of God, which is real love.[17] In
speaking of the prayer of petition, he distinguishes between
a humble, general request—*supplicatio*, a request for some
particular grace—*postulatio*, and an *insinuatio*, or 'suggestion',
such as Our Lady's intervention at Cana, or the message of
Martha and Mary: Lord, *he whom thou lovest is sick*.[18] Here the
soul simply lays bare its needs and leaves the issue to God.

---

[16] *De modo orandi*, Hugo S. Vict., t. III; c. 979; P. L., CLXXVI.
[17] *Summa Theol.*, IIa, IIæ, q. 82, art. 1. *Devotio non aliud esse videtur quam
voluntas quædam prompte tradendi se ad ea quæ pertinent ad Dei famulatum.*
[18] John 11:3.

Devotion, says Hugh, perfects prayer, and here we seem at last to emerge from the Purgative Way. He now speaks of 'pure prayer', and it is distinctly contemplative 'when from abundance of devotion the soul is so enkindled that when it turns to God to ask Him for something, on account of the greatness of its love, it even forgets its petition; and, for love of Him whom it sees, vehemently desiring to rejoice in Him, and yearning to rest wholly in Him, it freely lays aside all care of that for which it came. And as this kind of prayer is utterly unlike all others, so it is precious beyond all others in the sight of God'. Hugh says again: 'perfect prayer' is 'perfect love'.[19]

Students of St. John of the Cross will find no difficulty in recognizing where they are here. The hard period of the *Dark Night* of the senses is over, and although this prayer is still usually the 'loving attention' to which the soul has attained through its own efforts, aided throughout by the *gratia cooperans* which enables it to work *vitaliter et libere*[20]—in a manner which is vital and free, and so meritorious, something else is intervening, at least occasionally: something for which it can only prepare itself, but which God may well grant by a special grace to which it has no 'right' but for which it may well hope.

Prayer time is no longer taken up with preliminaries which, strictly, are not the prayer at all; remote preparation is relegated to other times, partly made by spiritual reading, and partly by that 'prayerfulness', that recollection, which can continue even amid daily duties. Such is the order of life in a fervent monastery and, *mutatis mutandis*, such is possible outside one.

Hugh wrote several smaller works on prayer, but these merely repeat his earlier teaching. He recognizes the sufferings and purifications undergone in what will later be called the *Nights* of the soul,[21] and in a book on the

---

[19] *De modo orandi*, Hugo S. Vict., t. III, col. 979 *seq.* and 984; P. L., CLXXVI.
[20] *Summa Theol.*, Ia, IIæ, q. III, art. 2.
[21] *De modo orandi*, col. 978; P. L., CLXXVI.

Church, *De arce Noë*, we read: 'Between the love of this
world and the love of God there is this difference: that
the love of this world seems sweet in the beginning, but
has a bitter ending, whereas the love of God begins in
bitterness, but its last end is full of sweetness.'[22] His *De
laude caritatis* is one long prayer in praise of divine love;
a prose equivalent to St. John's poem of the *Dark Night*.

A last work of general instruction upon the spiritual
life is the *Eruditionis Didascalicæ*.[23] There are five steps
whereby the soul is raised to perfection: (1) Reading or
doctrinal teaching, (2) meditation, (3) prayer, (4) work, (5)
contemplation. Each is higher than the preceding one,
and whilst the first is that of beginners, the fifth is that
of the perfect, who already taste in this life something
of the future reward of the good 'work' or holy living.

At the first stage, the soul receives instruction, thus
laying a firm foundation for all that follows; in meditation,
it receives counsel, and learns what it must do; in prayer
it begs for grace to carry out what it has learnt. It then
begins to work with the grace obtained, and the author
is emphatic when treating of co-operation with grace. 'If
you alone work, you do nothing; if God alone works, you
merit nothing.' Thus the soul continues to 'seeks' God
and at last, 'finds' Him in contemplation.[24]

Hugh's other works are concerned with contemplation
only, and on that subject he is at his best. We can parallel
many a passage with similar portions of the Spiritual Canticle and the *Living Flame of Love*, although further variations
occur in his nomenclature, seeing that he is still feeling his
way. Nevertheless, he writes with greater ease since, for the
most part, he is obviously drawing upon his own experience.

We may consider that the *Soliloquium de Arrha Animæ*,
known in an English translation as the *Soul's betrothal Gift*,
which is in the form of a dialogue between Man and his

---

[22] *De arca Noë*, c. 1, col. 619; *P. L.*, CLXXVI.
[23] *Erud. Didas.*, l. 5, c. 9; *P. L.*, CLXXVI.
[24] *De laude caritatis*, P. L., CLXXVI.

Soul: a somewhat artificial device, but one which does not affect the sublimity of the thought. *Anima* seeks instruction in the spiritual life from *Homo*. The soul mentions various difficulties, gives some account of its conduct and describes its prayer. The following passage occurs towards the end:

> Who is this who sometimes touches me and delights me so sweetly, and with such vehement tenderness, that I seem in a certain manner, to go out of myself, and know not to what I am drawn away. For suddenly I am renewed, and all is well with me beyond all I can say. My mind rejoices; I forget past sorrows; my consciousness is delighted; my understanding becomes clearer; my heart is overjoyed; my desires are satisfied; and I find myself borne away I know not whither, and embraced interiorly with the arms of love. I know not what it is, but I strive with all my heart to hold and never to lose it. My soul struggles to detain that which I long to embrace forever, lest it be withdrawn. Is this my Beloved?
>
> *Man.* Truly it is thy Beloved who visits thee, but He comes invisible and hidden. He comes incomprehensible; He comes that He may touch thee, not that He may be seen by thee; He comes to admonish thee, not that He may be grasped at by thee; He comes not that He may infuse Himself wholly into thee, but that He may offer Himself to thee to be tasted; not that He may fulfil thy desire, but that He may draw they affection. He offers thee, as it were, the first-fruits of love! He does not show thee the fulness of perfect fruition. And this is what supremely belongs to the pledge of thy betrothal: that He who in time to come will give Himself to be seen and possessed by thee forever, now sometimes offers Himself to be tasted, that thou mayest experience for thyself how sweet He is.

And again, *Homo* says: 'I know that thy life is love, and I know that without love thou couldst not be.'[25] We need

---

[25] *De Arrha Animæ* (II), col. 970; *P. L.*, CLXXVI.

only compare this with St. John's poem of the *Dark Night*, and that other: *I die because I cannot die*, to trace one of the Mystical Doctor's sources of inspiration.

The same work contains a remarkable passage which certainly found its way to Spain, for we find its teaching in the *Exercises* of St. Ignatius. *Homo* reminds *Anima* of all that God has done:

> And what if you begin to think how many gen-
> erations of men have passed from the beginning
> of the world until now...without the knowledge
> of God....To all of these your Redeemer and
> Lover preferred you, when He bestowed upon you
> this grace which none of them were entitled to
> receive. Why do you suppose you were preferred
> to all of them, that you, rather than they, were
> entitled to receive a special grace?...You alone
> are raised up in preference to all of them; no
> cause can you find except the freely given love of
> your Saviour. So He chose you, and singled you
> out; your Betrothed, your Lover, your Redeemer,
> your God. He chose you among them all, and
> raised you up from them all, and loved you before
> them all. He called you by His name, that there
> should be a memorial of Him always with you.
> He willed you to share in His name, to share
> in the truth of His name, inasmuch as He has
> anointed you with that oil of gladness where-
> with He Himself is anointed; so that He who
> is called 'Christian' by Christ shall be anointed
> by the Anointed.[26]

The treatise *De Anima* is a more didactic work. It considers God and our neighbour and, what is not very common at this date, the Mystical Body, and the work of the Blessed Sacrament in producing that unity of the faithful as members with the Head: 'By the partaking of

---

[26] *De Arrha Animæ*, Hugo S. Vict., t. II, col. 970, 963 and 951; *P. L.*, CLXXVI. Eng. Trans. by Professor Sherwood Taylor (Dacre Press, Westminster).

the Body and Blood of Christ, the Son of God, we are incorporated into His life'.[27]

Anon, Hugh returns to the subject of contemplation—or to be strictly accurate, of contemplative prayer, and emphasizes its power to purify and detach the soul. It is remarkable that, almost alone of mystical theologians except St. John of the Cross, he does not consider the trials as punitive, but as essentials of the state and 'constructive'.

> The grace of contemplation not only cleanses from every stain of worldliness, but also sanctifies the soul and sets it on fire with the love of heavenly good things. He who, thanks to the inspirations and lights of the Holy Spirit, has been raised to contemplation, receives the pledges of the future happiness wherein he will enjoy an eternal contemplation. But if anyone would be raised to the contemplation of the truth, he must abstain not only from evil works but even from useless thoughts. Many there are who keep themselves outwardly at rest, but who, because they cannot preserve tranquillity of heart, cannot be fulfilled in them the Psalmist's words: *Be still and see that I am God.*[28] Their bodies are at rest, but their hearts are agitated and dissipated among all kinds of objects, and therefore they cannot taste how sweet the Lord is. *How good is God to Israel: to them that are of a right heart!*[29]

Nothing is more agreeable, nothing more profitable than the grace of contemplation.... To know God is the fulness of knowledge, but to acquire this knowledge of God interior contemplation is more helpful than study; sighs more than reasonings, tears more than beautiful thoughts, prayer more than reading; to ponder upon heavenly things more than to be anxious over things of earth.[30]

---

[27] *De Anima*, Hugo S. Vict., *P. L.*, CLXXVI, and *Hom. I in Eccles.*, where there is a preface on the Blessed Sacrament.
[28] Psalm xlv. 11.
[29] Psalm lxxii. 1.
[30] *De Anima*, l. III, c. 49; *P. L.*, CLXXVI.

Much of the book is addressed directly to God, and even verbally closely resembles passages in St. John's later works. One feels the latter must have loved and absorbed many a sentence:

> I love Thee, O my God! I love Thee and I will to love Thee more and more. Grant, O Thou fairest among the sons of men, that I may desire Thee; that I may love Thee as much as I would and as I should. Thou art immense, and Thou shouldst be loved without measure;[31] above all, by us whom Thou hast so loved, so saved; for whom Thou hast done so much and such great things. O Love that ever burnest, and shalt never be extinguished; sweet Christ! good Jesus! supreme charity! My God! enkindle me wholly with love of Thee: that love which chooses Thee beyond all others;[32] with longing for Thee; with thy charity, thy joy and exultation; thy loving-kindness and thy gentleness; thy will and desiring, which is holy, chaste and pure; so that wholly filled with the sweetness of thy love, I may shed around me the fire of thy charity. May I love, my Lord, most sweet and most fair, with my whole heart, my whole soul, my whole strength, and my every intention.[33]

We have alluded to Hugh's devotion to the Blessed Sacrament; we may now note one of many expressions of his love of the sacred Humanity, and even an early example of devotion to the Sacred Heart.

> In the Saviour's wounds is perfect and enduring rest for the weak and for sinners. There I dwell securely. His heart lies open through His wounds. Whatever I lack, I draw for myself from the heart of my Lord; for it overflows with mercy; nor does the wound fail whence it flows. Through

---

[31] A reminiscence of St. Bernard.
[32] Hugh here uses both *amor* and *dilectio*.
[33] *De Anima*, l. IV, c. 6; *P. L.*, CLXXVI.

the wounds of His body, He opens to me the
secret place of His heart; He opens to me the
great symbol[34] of His tender mercy: the bowels
of the mercy of our God, in which the Orient
from on high hath visited us. The wounds of
Christ Jesus are full of mercy, full of tender love,
full of sweetness and charity.[35]

And again:

O my soul, signed with the image of God,
redeemed with the blood of Christ, espoused
to Him in faith, dowered by the Holy Spirit,
adorned with virtues ... love Him by whom
thou hast been so greatly loved. Look upon Him
who looks upon thee. Seek him who seeks thee.
Love thy Love by whom thou art loved, whose
love goes before thee and is the cause of thy
love. ... In the day of thy death, when all thy
friends will withdraw from thee, He will not
forsake thee but will keep thee safe from those
who are roaring and ready to devour thee, and
will guide thee through a path unknown and lead
thee to the streets of the Sion on high, and there
place thee, with the angels, before the face of His
Majesty. ... By love thou canst ascent, to the lover
nothing is difficult, nothing is impossible. The
soul that loves often ascends and runs familiarly
through the streets of the heavenly Jerusalem.[36]

Finally, in the *De laude caritatis*, we may single out a
few passages which illustrate Hugh's thought. The period
to which he belonged stands out for its devotion to the
person of Christ. It was a legacy from St. Bernard. Already,
also, in Hugh we meet with that 'grievous joy in the
holy Cross' which was to be such an outstanding feature
of the Franciscan spirituality in the next age. The book
in question is largely concerned with the sufferings of

---

[34] The Latin word is *sacramentum*.
[35] *De Anima*, l. IV, c. 10; *P. L.*, CLXXVI.
[36] *Ibid.*, c. 11, col. 132; *P. L.*, CLXXVI.

Christ, and it emphasizes the longing of the loving soul to suffer with Him in the spirit of St. Paul's: *That I may know Him, and the power of His resurrection: and the fellowship of His sufferings: being made conformable to His death.*[37] Love made Him leave His Father's throne to put on the vesture of our mortal flesh; love has wounded the impassible, bound the invincible, dragged along the immovable, subjected the Eternal to death!'[38] In this treatise also he treats of the divine indwelling of the Holy Spirit, and here it is noteworthy that he follows Peter Lombard in teaching the identity of the Holy Ghost and the charity received in the soul. Later theologians would differentiate between the created gift and the uncreated Giver.[39]

We may end on Hugh's words:

> It is by love that you set forth, by love that you attain.... Love is all for you. Love is the choice, it is the way, the attainment, the sojourning, the beatitude. Then love God, choose God, run, attain, possess and enjoy. The soul is transformed into the image of Him whom it loves.[40]

2. RICHARD OF ST. VICTOR

RICHARD OF ST. VICTOR HAS BEEN CALLED 'the spiritual master of the Middle Ages', and 'the first really theological writer on high spirituality'. Both claims are perhaps somewhat exaggerated, but from a theological point of view, although not from a literary one, his work marks a

---

[37] Phil. 3:10.

[38] *De laude caritatis*, col. 975; *P. L.*, CLXXVI.

[39] It is true, however, that charity cannot be possessed save by one in a state of grace, and that renders God present precisely as the object of our knowledge and love. St. Thomas corrects the earlier opinion, as he does so many others of the first scholastics. We can watch the development in this great mediæval period. 'The gifts of the Holy Spirit are connexes with the charity as infused habits, and grow with it.' (*Summa Theol.*, Ia, IIæ, q. 68, art. 5.) 'The Holy Spirit is not in a man without His gifts. Therefore His gifts abide in man. Therefore they are not merely acts or passions, but abiding habits.' (*Ibid.*, art. 3.)

[40] 4 *De laude caritatis*, *P. L.*, CLXXVI.

distinct advance upon that of Hugh. He is the latter's loyal disciple, accepts his definitions and does not differ markedly from him on the whole; but he is often over subtle, very prolix and his many divisions and sub-divisions frequently make him difficult to follow, whilst the style of his two greatest works, in particular, is artificial and over-symbolical. The verse: *Benjamin adolescentulus in mentis excessu*—'There is Benjamin, a youth in ecstasy of mind,' has suggested his titles; but once the reader can forget the often forced 'accommodation' of the Old Testament passages, he finds that he has before him, as has been said, a body of doctrine.[41]

We know little of the author himself. He was a Scotsman, and entered the abbey of St. Victor under its first abbot, Gilduin. He became a pupil of Hugh, and subsequently a learned philosopher and theologian, producing works on the Trinity, the Incarnation, the work of the Holy Spirit in the Church and on Our Lady; besides a commentary on the *Canticle of Canticles*, 'Annotations' on some Psalms, works on moral theology, etc. Some of his most valuable work on spiritual theology, as we shall see, is to be found in a couple of his shortest treatises.

Unlike Hugh, he devoted himself to strictly religious studies. Indeed, there is a reproachful allusion in *Benjamin Major* to such as 'in our times, as well as formerly, have chosen to follow Aristotle, but have become wiser and learnt to know Christ and Him crucified'.[42] He himself, however, 'loved reason with so intemperate a love that he actually undertook to explain even the mystery of the Trinity as a necessary truth demonstrable to conviction by human reason'.[43] About 1157, he became Sub-Prior and was subsequently Prior, but, distinguished as he was for piety and zeal, he had much to suffer, and we catch the echo of this experience in his works. Gilduin was succeeded as Abbot

---

[41] Psalm lxxviii, 28.
[42] *Ben. Maj.*, l, II, c. 1; *P. L.*, CXCVI.
[43] See *The Life of the Church*, P. III, 'Christianity in the Middle Ages', by P. Rousselot and P. Huby S. J. (Ed. by Fr. M. D'Arcy, S. J.).

by Ervisus, who, whatever he may have been when elected, developed into a thoroughly relaxed and unworthy Superior, who resisted all pressure to make him resign and finally had to be deposed by higher authority. In his work, *De gradibus caritatis*, which was written for a private friend, Richard writes sadly: "Those who come to this tomb of Christ, which is the cloister, find only the grave clothes; that is the uniformity of the habit. I own it is sad to be here'. He died on March 10, probably in 1173, and the following entry was inserted in the Necrology of St. Victor's: 'Today is the anniversary of Richard, Prior of this church; who, by his example of holy conversation[44] and the beauty of his writings left us when he died a worthy remembrance of his name'.

We have seen that although the earlier mediæval writers knew the general essentials of spiritual theology as well as their successors, from a practical standpoint their teaching is far from clear. They all imply that what is now known as infused contemplation and is the first form of prayer that is 'mystical', properly speaking, develops as a matter of course out of meditation, or at best out of affective prayer. This, experience must have shown, then as later, is far from being invariably the case, and the subject can neither produce the later form of prayer at will nor disperse it. Many souls never experience it at all, and others only after years. The outstanding contribution of Richard to the subject of prayer is that he plainly teaches the existence of another sort of contemplation, obtainable by the soul's own industry, aided by ordinary grace[45] and is thus the first to bridge the gap between discursive meditation and mystical contemplative prayer. Others must have recognized the *thing*—as we know several later authorities did—but they did not recognize that this, later to be called 'acquired', or 'beginners'' contemplation, was a definite form of prayer, differing from those which preceded and followed it, and

---

[44] *Conversatio* was for long the technical expression for the monastic life.
[45] *Ben. Maj.*, l. V, c. 1; *P. L.*, CXCVI.

marking a critical transition stage in the spiritual life during which souls need wise guidance.

It is usually stated that the treatise *Benjamin Minor* is ascetical and *Benjamin Major* mystical, but the last chapters of the former deal with contemplation, which as usual is not distinguished from contemplative prayer, so that the reader must make his own adjustments. Richard cites Hugh's definition of contemplation but is not quite satisfied with it, though his own is not satisfactory either. As St. Thomas points out, a definition depends upon the writer's personality and his state of soul. No mystic can be 'detached' as not to be influenced by his own experience.[46]

Richard is encouraging in that he urges all to strive after contemplation, which simply means striving after holiness of life, so is no special preserve of the few. Hugh and Guigo the Carthusian had adopted the simile of the ladder, Richard prefers that of the mountain. All can and should climb it, but few do so

> either because they will not or they cannot ascend so far. Very rare is it to ascend this mountain, but rarer still to stand and linger there, and rarest of all to dwell and rest there. Not only can this mountain not be climbed saving with great effort, but without great difficulty the soul cannot remain on the summit. But perhaps thou hast already ascended; perhaps thou art already standing there; yet that is not enough. Learn to remain and make thy dwelling there ... by detaching thy mind from everything whatsoever.[47]

> Whosoever thou art who would go up into this mountain, follow Christ. The way that leads to the summit ... is hard, secret, and unknown to many. I hold that those alone run without going astray, those alone reach it without hindrance, who follow Christ, who art led by the Truth. Whosoever thou art who dost make thy way to the heights,

---

[46] *Summa Theol.*, IIa, IIæ, q. 180, art. 6.
[47] *Ben. Min.*, c. 76, col. 54; *P. L.*, CXCVI.

thou mayest go securely if the Truth go before
thee; for otherwise thou labourest in vain.... [48]

Benjamin Minor is mostly concerned with the Purgative Way, and we have the usual exhortations to aim at
the different virtues, which are represented by Joseph,
who stands for the active, whereas Benjamin represents
the contemplative side of the spiritual life. Both are the
children of one mother, but Benjamin is born long after
his brother. Richard also uses the favourite comparison
of the mirror with the traditional application. He insists
strongly upon self-knowledge:

> In vain does he lift the eye of the heart to see
> God, who has not yet succeeded in seeing him-
> self. Let a man first learn to know his unseen
> self, before he presumes that he can understand
> the unseen things of God. If you cannot know
> yourself, how can you presume to understand
> those things which are above you?[49]

> Let whosoever thinks to see his God, wipe the
> mirror of his mind; let him cleanse his spirit.
> When he has wiped the mirror, and long and
> diligently looked into it, a certain brightness
> of divine light begins to shine through.... That
> light had shone into the eyes of him who said:
> *The light of thy countenance, O Lord, is signed upon us.*[50]
> Therefore, from the sight of this light, which it
> beholds with awe in itself, the soul is enkindled in
> a wonderful manner, and urged on to see the light
> which is above itself. From this vision, I say,[51]
> it conceives the flame of desire to see God and
> takes confidence. Therefore, let the soul which
> is now on fire with this longing, and already in
> hope, know that it has now conceived Benjamin
> whom it desires. For it conceives by hoping, and

---

[48] *Ibid.*, c. 77.
[49] *Ben. Min.*, c. 71, col. 15; *P. L.*, CXCVI.
[50] *Ben. Min.*, c. 72, col. 52, and Psalm iv. 6.
[51] *Visio* here does not mean 'vision', but merely an ordinary grace
of spiritual insight.

brings forth by desiring; and the more it desires
the nearer it is to bringing forth.[52]

But Benjamin's birth costs Rachael's life, and she dies
in suffering. Joseph stands for the meditation which is
concerned with right conduct: acquiring, preserving and
increasing true good things; Benjamin is the contemplation
which is concerned with invisible things. Just as meditation may rise to contemplation, so the latter may descend
again to meditation. The soul suffers from seeing its hope
deferred, but it must be patient and not relax. It seems
here that Richard is thinking of the 'active', or 'acquired',
contemplation to which he has already referred. We meet
the fluctuations when meditation is being replaced by a
simpler form of prayer; the difficulty of simply 'going on'
when, as St. Teresa puts it, the 'water' of the contemplative prayer is being doled out only by 'mouthfuls'; and, as
Richard mentions in another work,[53] the aridity which is
yet accompanied by intense longing for God, whom the
soul does not feel although He is there: all these the Carmelite Doctor will enumerate and explain centuries later.

We turn now to *Benjamin Major*, which opens with
some recapitulation of Richard's earlier teaching. Prayer
is divided into *cogitatio*, 'which is the mind's glance and
prone to wander'; meditation, which is the searching
for truth or, to cite St. Thomas, who takes the passage
from Richard, 'the survey of the mind whilst occupied in
searching for truth',[54] and contemplation, which is the 'the
soul's clear and free dwelling upon the object of its gaze'.
This last definition is found also in Hugh of St. Victor.[55]

Meditation is an 'arduous and sharp' process, carried
on with great industry, whereas in contemplation the soul
takes flight freely and is borne away, hither and thither,
with wonderful agility, wherever the impetus (of the Holy

---

[52] *Ben. Min.*, c. 72, col. 52; *P. L.*, CXCVI.
[53] *Comm. in Cant.*, c. 35; *P. L.*, CXCVI.
[54] *De Trin.*, l. XV, c. 8. *Summa Theol.*, IIa, IIæ, q. 180, art. 3.
[55] Hugo S. Vict., *Hom. 1 in Eccles.*; *P. L.*, CLXXXV.

Spirit) carries it.[56] In cogitation there is neither labour
nor fruition; in meditation there is both, whilst in contemplation there is fruition without labour.

Contemplation may be concerned with what is above
reason but not contrary to reason, or with what is both
above and contrary to reason. The Blessed Trinity is an
example of the latter (though the author's views seem to
have varied at different times); as also are many things
about Our Lord, such, for instance, as His presence in the
Blessed Sacrament. In this life, there are three stages in
our knowledge of God, which may be likened to the three
heavens: God may be seen by faith, known by knowledge,
and perceived by contemplation. To the first two men
attain by their own efforts, aided by ordinary grace, but
to the third heaven the soul cannot rise itself but must
be 'rapt' or carried out of itself.

Here it is well to distinguish, as do mediæval authors,
between ecstasy and rapture. In the latter case a certain
violence is implied, so that the soul is seized upon suddenly,
whether during actual prayer or outside of such times.
Although certain external features are associated with
such a state in later times, the context of many passages
in earlier mediæval works shows that such concomitants
were not necessarily included.

Richard states, as do others, that we ascend to things
invisible by means of things visible, and that the same
material is used in contemplation as in meditation, only
it is used differently. At first the imagination is much
used, but as the soul progresses, normally it is used less.
As Richard himself says, by meditating we pass beyond
meditation and cross the boundary into contemplation.
After some time, longer or shorter, there is no need to
think over in detail, e.g., an incident in the Gospel, or any
similar subject of meditation. From practice, the person
is familiar with it, and takes it in 'at a glance'—syntheti-
cally—and this marks the beginning of what the Victorines

---

[56] *Ben. Maj.*, l. I, c. 4; *P. L.*, CXCVI.

and mediæval writers generally call 'contemplation'. The prayer itself at this stage takes the form of the 'loving attention' already mentioned. At times, as Richard teaches, the soul is 'held in admiration'—silent before God—and then what St. Teresa calls 'mouthfuls' of infused contemplation—Prayer of Quiet—may be granted if God wills 'to raise the soul above itself', as Denys and all the rest express it. This last seems to be the fourth stage; the fifth corresponds to the prayer of Union, when the Quietude has become a *state*, and the sixth is the last stage in this life: the Transforming union. Richard says that for the soul at these later stages the proper subject of contemplation is the Trinity, and all mystical writers follow him. It is a fact, easily verified by reading the lives of canonized saints and of such as may be 'canonizable', that a strong devotion to the Blessed Trinity develops steadily as the spiritual life progresses; and towards the end, when the divine masterpiece is complete, there is sometimes some experimental realization of the in-dwelling of the three divine Persons in the soul.

The fourth stage is the 'second heaven' in which Richard recognizes a definite action of the gifts of the Holy Spirit. In the last two, which constitute the 'third heaven': 'our ark is carried up into the Holy of Holies'. It is interesting that very occasionally, Richard uses the ancient word *theoria*, which in early times stood for infused, mystical prayer, but became almost obsolete later.

However, he wisely reminds his readers that, no matter what stage they may have reached, they must not neglect spiritual reading, or fail to accept any teaching God may send them. 'Every day we learn new things from the Scriptures. Often some text tells us much in a word or two—*multum in unum*. God sends His messengers, teaching us what our Beloved wills us to do, reminding us of what He has done, and setting before us what He is yet prepared to do for us.'[57]

---

[57] *Ben. Maj.*, l. IV, c. 14; *P. L.*, CXCVI.

Yet few correct their lukewarmness, and we have some warnings probably suggested by the unsatisfactory state of the writer's own monastery at the time of writing. *Lectio divina* must be what its name implies, and not merely study for its own sake. 'They thirst after what they may boast about, not after that whereby they may be edified. They love learning, not holiness.'[58] There are others who, notwithstanding real labour and sincerity, so far as can be judged, do not attain to contemplative prayer,[59] and probably Richard would have remarked of these, as does St. John of the Cross: 'God alone knoweth why!'[60] There are many who think they are prepared, who yet fall short of what God requires, owing to cowardice or want of detachment; and here, again, we might be listening to the Carmelite. 'If you seek or receive consolation outside of God, you do not yet love Him alone, even although you may love Him much.'[61] 'It is hard to be utterly detached from self and from all else.'[62] We who are in earnest must busy ourselves—*satagimus*—in loving God intimately and supremely, and earnestly desire the joy of divine contemplation. In another work, Richard treats of the same subject, and gives another wise word of warning, namely, that a contemplative must not, on the pretext of giving himself to prayer, neglect the duties of fraternal charity.[63]

We have further teaching in his Commentary upon the *Canticle of Canticles*.[64] Like Hugh and St. John, he speaks of the purifying side of contemplative prayer, namely, the characteristic aridity of the early stage, and perhaps has also in mind the later Night of the Spirit. The mountain of God is 'the mountain of myrrh' and He allows bitterness and suffering during the ascent. Nor does Richard connect

---

[58] *Ibid.*
[59] *Ibid.*
[60] *Living Flame of Love*, S. III (B).
[61] *Ben. Maj.*, l. IV, c. 15.
[62] *Ben. Maj.*, l. IV, c. 14.
[63] *Annotatio* in Psalm xxiv.; *P. L.*, CXCVI.
[64] *Expos. in Cant.*, c. 25; *P. L.*, CXCVI.

such suffering with some lapse into sin, or regard it as a sign of divine displeasure. On the contrary, it is the work of God, and destined to do great things in the soul.[65]

In his commentaries on the Psalms, he returns to the subject of the 'three heavens', but treats it differently. The characteristic of the first is contemplation of the truth; of the second, the love of justice, and of the third fullness of eternal joy. If a man is not in the first, wherein he firmly believes God's truth, he is not a Catholic; if he is not in the second, he is not a good man; if he is in both, then as St. Paul says, his conversation is in heaven. In the third, however, he must be carried, for he cannot enter by himself. The soul is admitted therein as often as by *excessu mentis*—ecstasy, it is granted fruition in some part of that inner and eternal sweetness. A soul is thus rapt into this third heaven when the sea of eternal happiness engulfs it, so that not only does it cease to remember all external things, but it comes to forget its very self. 'Brother, if the light of truth shines around thee, thou holdest the first heaven; if the flame of love burns within thee, the second; if thou hast experienced a certain touch of interior sweetness, thou hast been admitted to the third.'[66]

Richard teaches, moreover, that at no stage is the Sacred Humanity to be left out, although, as has been well said, the danger of souls so doing is not really very likely. In practice, earnest people find no difficulty in reconciling, e.g., devotion to the Trinity with devotion to Our Lord. Always He is *'Jesus-who-is-God'*.[67]

So much for Richard's greater treatises, but in a small work we find him writing of contemplative prayer in a way that may well surprise us, for St. Teresa's Spiritual Castle is the lineal descendant of his *De quatuor gradibus violentiæ caritatis*. The elements of mystical contemplation are these:

---

[65] *Ibid.*, cc. 19 and 25; *P. L.*, CXCVI.
[66] *Annotatio* in Psalm cxxi.
[67] *The Spiritual Director, according to the Principles of St. John of the Cross*, by Fr. Gabriel of St. Mary Magdalen, O. D. C., Mercier, Cork, 1952.

infused light, infused love, and a special working of the
Holy Spirit in the soul; any action on the senses, whether
of joy or suffering, is secondary. He distinguished four
stages: in the first, love penetrates the will; in the second,
it becomes all-embracing, and penetrates the understanding also; in the third, love becomes 'tyrannical'; that means
the soul rejects everything else, is in a state of utter desire,
and gives all for love. Then follows a fourth stage when
the lover puts himself forever at Love's service. It is a
state of utter giving.

The first stage is that of the Quietude which has
captivated the will, but not the understanding. To St.
Teresa this is the first stage of real contemplation. St.
John allows the term to the preceding stage—acquired
contemplation—but Richard will not allow that the prayer
is truly contemplation so long as the understanding is
not dominated. At this stage—again a little later than St.
John—he places the passive *Night of Sense*. There Israel is
in the desert, for the soul must be deprived of the food
it enjoyed in Egypt: that is of sensible sweetness and
facility in prayer. But God visits it from time to time,
and gives it grace to persevere, so that it rises to what,
for Richard, is at last real mystical contemplation, but for
Teresa and John is the Prayer of Union. At this stage, it
experiences joy, and also a deeper and more enlightened
grasp of the truths of faith. We have here the two kinds
of contemplation in which love and light, respectively
predominate—the 'Seraphic' and the 'Cherubic' to use a
traditional distinction—and which in the case of a saint
become eventually one.

The next stage is ecstatic union, and, like all other
spiritual theologians, Richard says that this does not last
long at a time, at least in its intensity. It corresponds to
St. Teresa's Fifth Mansion, and Richard says, with her,
that although the soul cannot remember afterwards all
that it has learnt in the period of ecstatic prayer, it has
no doubt whatever that it has been with God. Ecstasy is

caused by light, love and joy, and the senses are temporarily hindered from working, but there need not be any external phenomena which attract the attention of onlookers.

Now comes the *Dark Night of the Spirit*, and Richard uses a simile later borrowed by St. John of the Cross: no longer a log, but a piece of iron in a fire.[68] The metal, at first black, becomes glowing and finally liquifies. So the soul is made one spirit with God, and 'languishes' for Him. Cleansed from its last imperfections, after intense but fruitful suffering, it reaches the last stage: Transforming union. *To me to live is Christ.* It is wholly occupied in the service of love; it practises virtue in an heroic degree; it longs to suffer for God; it loves sinners as He loves them, and longs for their salvation. It becomes intensely apostolic yet is ever in peace.

We may note a last characteristic, which reminds us not only of St. John of the Cross but of St. Bonaventure, and practically all the mystics of the old Orders: namely his urgent exhortations to all to strive after sanctity, to aim at reaching intimate union with God, to fit themselves, so far as in them lies, to receive those higher graces of prayer which He may well give them, even though He has not bound Himself to do so. As says St. John: God is seeking the soul far more than it is seeking Him,[69] and it is not His fault if far more souls do not reach the heights. We should aspire 'obstinately' to divine contemplation, and set ourselves to do our part in every place and at all times.[70] We must 'stretch out our hearts by desire and await at every hour—what say I? at every moment—the coming of divine revelation.'[71] So far, all we have read applies to all souls of good will, and like the reply of St. Thomas Aquinas to his sister Theodora's

---

[68] *Dark Night*, B. II, c. 10, St. John uses both similes simultaneously, thus borrowing from both Hugh and Richard, but evidently quoting from memory.
[69] *Living Flame of Love*, (B), c. 3, n. 28.
[70] *Ben. Maj.*, l. IV, c. 10.
[71] *Ibid.*

enquiry as to how one becomes a saint, can be summed
up in the word: *Velle*—Will it! When Richard comes to
treat of religious, in whose case to love God as perfectly as
possible, and to aim at real holiness, is a debt of honour,
he speaks more strongly still: 'But what shall we say of
those of us who have received the religious habit, who are
formally bound to spiritual exercises, who are continually
receiving tokens of divine love; of us, who have no other
office assigned to us save to read, to sing psalms, to pray,
to meditate, to seek God, and to contemplate Him?'[72]
He enters into practical details for, like all true mystics,
he has his feet on the ground. The perfect religious is
rarely out of choir; he has no exceptions in the refectory;
only obedience sends him into the infirmary and keeps
him there;[73] he attributes no good that may be in him
to himself.[74] And once more, the reader is exhorted to
detachment: 'We know that a very great love admits of
no partners, accepts no rival.'[75]

We may recall that impassioned outburst of St. John:

> O souls created for these great things and called
> thereto! What are you doing? Wherein do you
> occupy yourselves? Your desires are meanness,
> and your possessions miseries. O wretched blind-
> ness of the eyes of the souls, which are blind to
> so great a light, and deaf to so clear a voice; see-
> ing that as long as you seek grandeurs and glories
> you remain miserable and mean, and have become
> ignorant and unworthy of so many blessings![76]

---

[72] *Ibid.*, c. 14.
[73] *Expos. in Cant.*, c. 30.
[74] *Ibid.*, c. 31.
[75] *Ben. Maj.*, l. IV, c. 15.
[76] *Spirit. Cant.* (B), S. 39 (Peers trans.).

III

SAINT BONAVENTURE

'THE GLORIOUS DOCTOR, SAINT Bonaventure' is singled out for special study in the *Instruction for Novices*, signed by St. John of the Cross, as Consultor, on January 11, 1590, the only other writers mentioned by name being St. Teresa and the Dominican, Fr. Luis of Granada. So, from the first, the Carmelite reform was prepared to seek guidance from other religious Orders, and certainly the first novice master was the last man to prescribe for his disciples anything which he had not thoroughly studied and approved himself. We must now see what he expected his novices to learn from the Doctor *Seraphic*.

It must be borne in mind, however, that in the sixteenth century a number of works were ascribed to the latter which later research has decided are not his. Indeed, any mediæval book of which the author was not certainly known seems usually to have been fathered either upon him or upon St. Bernard; whilst to the last was assigned Bonaventure's treatise on the Passion, better known as the *Vitis Mystica*—the 'True Vine'. Consequently, we shall have to treat of the more important writings which constitute this Pseudo-Bonaventure. Again, certain portions of the Doctor's works have been inserted bodily into some well-known mediæval productions which, long considered original, are now known to be compilations or anthologies from several other authors. A well-known example is the *De Adhaerendo Deo*, which contains a whole chapter taken from St. Bonaventure's *Itinierarium mentis ad Deum*.

The main facts in the saint's life are fairly well known. John of Fidanza, to give him his real name, was born at Bagnoræa, near Viterbo, in 1221. Somehow, his name became changed into 'Bonaventure' but we know not why, for a

charming legend of St. Francis himself having used it is
mythical. From Bonaventure himself, we learn that he was
saved from death through the prayer of Francis, but, again,
we know not whether in the latter's lifetime or not. We
know nothing of his childhood, nor the exact date of his
entry into the Franciscan Order: 1238 and 1243 have both
been suggested, and scholars seem to prefer the later year.
From the Roman Province, he was sent to Paris to study
under the Englishman, Alexander of Hales, and in 1248
obtained his Licentiate to teach as Bachelor. This he did
with great success until 1255, when his career was inter-
rupted owing to the uproar caused by William de Saint
Amour and the secular doctors of Paris against the Mendicant schools and professors, and certain privileges enjoyed
by these comparatively new religious Orders. After the
Council of Anagni, and the condemnation of William's book,
The Perils of these last Times, by Alexander IV, Bonaventure
returned to Paris, and he and Thomas of Aquino received
the doctorate together in October 1257. In the same year,
though not turned thirty-six, Bonaventure was elected
Minister-General of his Order, which was going through
difficult times owing to the thorny questions raised by
the party of the *Spirituals*. The actual controversy need not
concern us here, but so successfully did the new General
acquit himself in his difficult office that he is known as 'the
second Founder' of the Friars Minor. In 1265, Clement IV
nominated him Archbishop of York, but the saint managed
to decline the honour. In 1273 he was consecrated Bishop
of Albano and created a cardinal by Gregory X, and in the
following year, together with Thomas Aquinas, he was sum-
moned to the General Council at Lyons; but for both the
great Doctors and saints, the end was close at hand. Thomas
died in March 1274, on his way thither, and Bonaventure in
July of the same year. He was buried at Lyons, the Dominican Peter of Tarentaise, later Pope Innocent V, preaching
the funeral sermon. Sixtus IV canonized him in 1482, and
Sixtus V declared him a Doctor of the Church.

Leo XIII called St. Bonaventure 'the Prince of Mystics'. Not only his own sanctity, but his wide experience and responsibility with religious at every stage of their careers, besides his many secular spiritual connections, admirably fitted him to write authoritatively upon the spiritual life. His purely mystical works are not many, but his so-called non-mystical books are full of spiritual theology, even when he sets out to write ostensibly upon something else. The following works are usually reckoned as mystical: the *Itinerarium mentis ad Deum, the De Triplici via, the Soliloquium, De sex Alis Seraphim, Vitis mystica, Lignum Vitæ, De perfectione vitæ, or animæ, the Collationes in Hexæmeron* and the *Collationes de Septem Donis Spiritus Sancti.* Besides these, we find much of his mystical teaching in his *Commentary on the Sentences,* the *Commentary on St. Luke,* and certain sermons.

Several of his works were translated into Spanish, as were books wrongly assigned to him, even in the lifetime of St. John of the Cross, so that the novices of Pastrana and Carmelites generally had access to them in the vernacular as well as in the original. There were three translations of the *Lignum Vitæ,* published respectively at Valladolid in 1512, Sarragossa in 1576 and Valencia in 1588, the second being by a Franciscan. The *Soliloquium* appeared in Spanish at Sarragossa in 1580, and the *Regula Novitiorum* in 1588 at Valencia. That the Seraphic Doctor continued to enjoy his privileged position after St. John's death, is clear from the fact that the latter's erstwhile novices continued to translate the genuine and what they believed to be the genuine works of *El glorioso Doctor.* The ill-fated Fr. Jerome Gracian translated the *De mystica Theologia,* of which we shall have more to say later, and it was published at Madrid in 1607, whilst some other works of the pseudo-Bonaventure were done into Spanish after St. John's death. As regards these latter, it must be remarked that, although 'spurious' in the sense that the Saint is not their author, in themselves, almost without exception, they are valuable, and often very beautiful. The

best were written by men in close contact with him, and
trained along his lines. In several cases, the matter was
apparently taken down by his hearers, or written out from
memory afterwards; hence in substance they give us their
Master's teaching, and one or two treatises seem likely to
have been written by his order.

With St. Bonaventure, we have a complete, orderly,
detailed study of the spiritual life, and realize that we
have come to the golden age of Scholasticism. Words now
familiar in mystical theology come into use for the first
time, although the saint is a great traditionalist. There is
much dividing and sub-dividing, however, which sometimes makes him not too easy to follow. At first sight, it
may seem surprising that St. John, a Thomist and trained
in an Order which had definitely ranged itself on the side
of the Angel of the Schools in the Thomist revival then
going on in Spain, should have yet set his disciples to
study the great genius on the 'other side'; but in the lifetime of the saints the differences between the theological
positions of their Orders were less accentuated than they
became later, when some Scotists and Thomists became
figuratively at daggers drawn. For the purpose for which
St. John prescribed his works, St. Bonaventure served
excellently, and there was nothing on the other side which
exactly met the need. As a modern Thomist scholar has
written: 'As regards abundance of matter, brilliance and
originality of style, Bonaventure is superior to Thomas.
In the case of the latter, the kind of language used corresponds to the calm reflection of the Aristotelian method;
in the former, on the other hand, the mode of expression
takes on the ardour proper to the Platonic-Augustinian
enthusiasm.'[1] Later on, after the Angelic Doctor had been
defended against attacks from the other side, and the
General Chapter of 1309 held, by the way, at Sarragossa,
had laid down that his teaching should be the *norma* in

---

[1] See M. Grabmann, *St. Thomas Aquinas: His Personality and Thought*
(Eng. trans. 1928).

the studies of his Order, his influence gradually came to surpass that of Bonaventure, and the German mystical school, which undoubtedly influenced St. John of the Cross, rested its teaching on 'the clear light, the dear Saint Thomas, the Master', as Suso calls him. True, in treating of contemplation, Bonaventure, as his brethren, maintains the primacy of the will over the intellect; but since St. Thomas teaches that though the contemplative life, as regards the essence of the action, pertains to the intellect, and as regards the motive cause of the exercise of that action it belongs to the will,[2] there was no need to argue on that score.

St. Bonaventure is the most conspicuous representative of the mysticism of the Scholastic age, says a modern Spanish scholar. 'The starting point of his mystical teaching is original sin. Man was created to contemplate truth directly, without labour, and clearly, but Adam's sin made this immediate contemplation impossible, since his faculties are clouded from the beginning and are not as God gave them. Intellectual labour, hard and incomplete, is insufficient to gain complete knowledge of the truth, and the most perfect means possible is love, which as far as can be, brings man back to the state in which God created him. Hence this return to God is a journey of the soul—an *Itinerarium mentis ad Deum.*'[3]

We find Bonaventure's scheme of spiritual life in the *Sentences*. The Redemption restores to man the possibility of that union with God lost by sin but, as we are weakened as a result of the fall, our part is difficult. The indwelling of the Holy Spirit assimilates us to the Blessed Trinity, and finally sanctifying grace 're-makes' it to that same image of the Trinity.[4] It belongs to grace to reform, to quicken, to enlighten, to assimilate, unite, stabilize and

---

[2] *Summa Theol.*, IIa, IIæ q, 180, art. 1-2.
[3] *Introducción a la Historia de la Literatura Mística en España*, Pedro Sainz Rodriguez. (Madrid, Editorial Voluntad, 1927.)
[4] *Breviloquium*, pars. V, c. 1.

to make acceptable and raise on high. Grace is a formal
participation in the divine nature, making the soul the
abode of the Trinity and the privileged bride of the Holy
Spirit.[5] We have precisely the same teaching from St. John
of the Cross in his *Spiritual Canticle*, and both teach the
same with respect to the work of the theological virtues.
These rectify understanding, memory and will, by ordain-
ing them directly to the Trinity, and thus they rule the
entire contemplative life. Finally, the soul is healed of
its wounds by the grace of the Sacraments.[6] According
to John, the abnegation and detachment necessary for
intimate union with God is brought about precisely by
those virtues, and, like the Victorines and Bonaventure, he
leads the soul at the end to the Blessed Trinity. Like his
predecessors, he holds that the latter is the proper object
of contemplation of those in the Unitive Way, and for
him, as for Bonaventure, the whole tremendous scheme
of sanctification rests upon the truth that by grace we
are made *partakers of the divine nature*.[7]

Bonaventure distinguishes the classical three Ways:
the Purgative Way leads to peace; the Illuminative leads
to truth and the Unitive Way leads to love.[8] He makes it
clearer than previous writers that these three states are not,
as Pseudo-Denys understands them, degrees of initiation,
but that they overlap and that the exercises prescribed
are needed simultaneously at every stage of the spiritual
life. The first is concerned with the expulsion of sin, the
second with the imitation of Christ and the third with
'the reception of the Bridegroom'. In the first two, the
soul is predominantly active, in the third predominantly
passive, and he allows that in this last, meditation scarcely
exists, having become unnecessary. He classifies prayer into
the usual *Meditation*, with which he couples *Reading*—the

---

[5] *II Sent.*, d. 29, a. 1. q. 5.
[6] *Breviloquium*, pars. V, c. 4.
[7] *Ascent of Mount Carmel*, B. II, c. 6, and B. III. II Peter i. 4.
[8] *De triplici via*, c. 1. It has often been wrongly called the *Incendium amoris*.

classical *lectio divina*—*Prayer*, and *Contemplation*, though he
never defines this last, save in so far as he cites the definition of Hugh of St. Victor. He breaks new ground in his
teaching as to mental and vocal prayer, and evidently takes
the former in the sense used by later writers and nowadays.
'In mental prayer the lips move not, but the heart speaks to
God.'[9] Mental prayer is the higher form, and vocal prayer
is ordained to it. It is made 'with pure and tender sighing
of the heart to God'.[10] In the case of less perfect souls,
mental prayer may be helped by vocal prayer but, on the
contrary, it may more often be hindered. In the latter case,
the vocal prayer should be dropped, and the soul should
give itself to mental prayer. Of course, this rule applies to
private prayer only; for vocal prayer recited in common,
above all the Divine Office, which is its highest form, must
be performed faithfully and as perfectly as possible. This is,
firstly, because religious in choir are carrying out on earth
what the angels and saints do in heaven; secondly, because
at each Hour we honour some phase or event of Our Lord's
life, and give thanks to God for His benefits. Further, the
Office is the setting for the Mass; we nourish our own
souls by it, and are moved to greater fervour. Finally, the
simple faithful, who come to our churches, are edified, and
helped to pray regularly and at fixed hours, when they see
and hear the Brethren in choir.[11]

Turning to consider the saint's works, we may begin
with the *De Triplici Via*, which has been called 'a little
summa of mystical theology.'[12] It is a short book, consisting of a Prologue and three chapters, and has an additional
interest in that Savonarola wrote a commentary upon it.
The author says he is not writing for great theologians,
but for the simple and unlearned: 'for those who are

---

[9] *Sent.* IV, d. 15, par. 2, art. 2.
[10] *Sermo de modo vivendi.*
[11] *De sex alis Seraphim*, c. 8.
[12] Unfortunately, this became a favourite title for works dealing
with the Three Ways, and there are at least two others extant
neither of which was written by Bonaventure.

striving to love God, rather than to know many things.'
'The art of loving God is learned by practising love, not
by disputation.' What he is here expounding, cannot be
grasped by those who are versed in the highest learning,
but are inferior in love. Such must first lay aside and
forget all that pertains to this world; shun earthly honours, and hate all ostentatious display of learning and
vain glory. Then they must betake themselves to most
high poverty, to prayer and meditation. If they do this,
the divine 'spark'—*scintilla*—will increase, and they will
be raised to a love which will enable them to transcend
all earthly things. They would be fitter instruments for
grace thus to work upon if they truly despised themselves,
and rejoiced to be despised by others.

In the Purgative Way, the soul sets about active purification, and, in meditation at this stage, reason, synderesis
and conscience all take part.[13] With Richard of St. Victor,
Bonaventure emphasizes the necessity of self-knowledge,
and he explains how each of these three does its share. Reason tells the man what must happen to one who violates
the temple of God; synderesis lets him know that such a
one must either be lost or cleansed by penance; conscience,
which is to synderesis as act is to habit, brings his guilt
home to him personally; then the will decides to repent
and amend.[14] In meditation, the soul is to examine itself as
to all its past sins, both of commission and omission, and

---

[13] This Scholastic word is used frequently by St. Bonaventure
and later mystical authorities. It is thus defined by St. Thomas:
'Synderesis is said to be the law of our mind; because it is a habit
containing the precepts of the natural law, which are the first
principles of human actions.' (*Summa Theol.*, IIa, IIæ, q. 94, art. 1.)

St. Bonaventure's own definition is: A motive power of the
soul, naturally moving and stimulating it towards what is good and
shrinking from what is evil, and in these respects it never errs;
neither is it in accordance with synderesis to sin. (*Compendium
Theologicæ veritatis*, l. II, 51.)

The office of Synderesis is to protest against evil and stimulate
to good. (*Ibid.*)

[14] *De Trip. Via.*, c. 1.

as to whether it has given way to *acedia*, that 'weariness in
well-doing' of which the ages of faith wisely took cogni-
zance, which is the cause of so much relaxation whether
in religious or devout people in the world, and to which
Bonaventure traces serious sins. This done, the soul must
rouse itself, restrain itself by mortification, and cultivate
interior joy—a typical Franciscan touch! It must turn to
prayer, which is one of the principal exercises of sanctifying grace,[15] and contains three elements: we deplore our
spiritual wretchedness, beg for God's mercy and adore Him
with *Latria*—the worship which is His due, and all prayer
must contain these elements. For this, we need His grace,
but He will give us that if we be sincerely humble and
penitent. We must also think upon the life of Our Lord,
using the imagination if it helps us, and remember that
the Holy Spirit is ever asking for us the graces we need.
The result of all this should be joy and *ecstasy*. Here we
meet the old difficulty. St. Bonaventure, like others, rather
leaves the impression that provided the soul perseveres it
can count upon receiving the highest mystical graces; but
he draws no distinction between the forms its prayer may
take at different stages, although he does allow that such
forms depend upon which of the three ways it is travers-
ing.[16] Evidently he assumes that the confessor will apply
the general teaching as required by the penitent.

Once in the Illuminate Way, the soul must try to learn
more and more of Our Lord and to follow Him ever
more faithfully. The subjects for meditation should be
the Incarnation, the Eucharist, the Holy Spirit, and the
mystery of the divine adoption. Those at this stage find
that they are gaining a new and better understanding of
the Scriptures and that devotion is enkindled.[17] At this

---

[15] *Breviloquium, pars.* V, c. 10.
[16] *De Trip. Via.,* c. 1.
[17] The saint uses the word differently from St. Thomas. The latter
says: Devotion is an act of the will, to the effect that a man sur-
renders himself readily to the service of God. (*Summa Theol.,* IIa,
IIæ, q. 82, art. 3.) Bonaventure sometimes identifies it with prayer

stage, the gifts of the Holy Ghost play a very important part, and the soul develops a living faith in the Incarnation and Redemption which arouses an ever-deepening love. It is crucified to the world, and would wish to die for the world if thereby any soul might love God. Such, says the saint, is perfect love, and no soul is perfect until this stage is reached. To this degree of love for his neighbour no man comes until he has first reached the perfect love of God, for whose sake he loves his neighbour. Such a one gives himself to 'holy meditations' on the love of God, keeping a perpetual sabbath with Him; he hungers for God, and all else merely wearies him. He delights in sufferings, contempt, and corporal penance; though now less from the desire to atone for his past sins, than in order to be like his Saviour. Such love of God carries him out of himself, and we have ecstasy in the accepted sense. The soul then rests in 'a sleep and silence' which nothing can disturb. Such as have reached this state do easily all that is perfect, whether it be to do or to suffer, to live or to die. There is no need to stress the similarity of this description to what St. John teaches of souls at the end of the Illuminative Way.

We come now to those in the Unitive Way, which leads to perfect charity and mystical wisdom. The soul is passive beneath the action of grace, and all its spiritual exercises are aimed at developing and purifying its love of God. As to its mediation, it is recollected and fixed in adoration, but here the prayer is infused, and obviously different from the adoration mentioned at the earlier stages. This prayer has three movements: the heart turns within to reverence and adore; it is dilated, so that it bursts into thanksgiving, and it is filled with the love of benevolence and raised above itself, so that it delights in that communing with God: 'as between bride and

---

and describes it as affective in character (*De sex alis seraphim*, c. 7). Again, it is a tender affective love, arising from the memory of God's loving-kindness to us. (*Coll. XII in Joan.; Sermo de S. Maria-Magdalena.*)

bridegroom.' The whole soul rejoices in God and in his good pleasure; it delights only in pleasing Him, and would have all men do likewise. 'This is the state and degree of perfect charity, and until it has been reached, no man should think himself perfect.' It is noteworthy that there is no mention of extraordinary graces, and, long before St. John of the Cross, the Seraphic Doctor warns his readers not to desire visions and revelations, which should rather be feared.[18] What is emphasized is the essential: the unity of absolute conformity between the divine will and that of the soul. 'That,' says St. Teresa, 'is the union which I have always desired, and never cease to ask from God, for it is the surest and safest.'[19] It is the 'transformation of love', described by St. John of the Cross.[20]

And, like St. John, St. Bonaventure maintains that to this union all souls may aspire, if they be willing to do their part and pay the price. It is rare only *de facto*, not *de jure*.

Not even at this stage must the soul forsake consideration of the Passion, though now it will take a rather different form,[21] and, a true son of St. Francis, Bonaventure still exhorts those in these later 'mansions' to let the beauty and wonder of creation move them to adore the Creator. And, as with all the great mystical writers, he ends with the Trinity, to which the sacred Humanity has been the 'bridge', as said St. Catherine of Siena. He closes on that note: Power, Wisdom, Love: God living in an eternal present: absolutely simple, and the soul crying: 'I seek Thee; I hope in Thee, I desire Thee; I receive Thee; I trust in Thee; I exult in Thee, and I cling to Thee!'

---

[18] *Sent.*, d. 23, art. 2, q. 3; and d. 9, art. 1, q. 6. *Coll. in Hex.* XXII, n. 42.

[19] *Int. Castle*, M.V., c. 3, n. 5.

[20] *Living Flame*, c. 3, n. 24; *Cant.* (A) S. 59.

[21] This is well expressed by Abbot Marmion, in his *Union with God* (see note on p. 186 of chapter V). 'When you are aware that a gentle peace is taking possession of your soul, be content to remain there in silent love, and *let God act.* It is not surprising that what once filled you with (sensible) devotion, such as the Passion, no longer affects you. That will come back, but *in another way.*'

A distinguished Franciscan scholar has pointed out[22] that Bonaventure treats of two kinds of contemplation: intellectual and 'sapiential'. We have seen that he is not the first to do so, but he is clearer than the Victorines. The latter is the higher, but the two merge in the end. As the soul draws nearer to God, we find ourselves no longer able to dissect it and analyse; it is taking on something of God's simplicity, so that we find ourselves synthesizing!

The *Itinerarium Mentis ad Deum* appeared in 1259, and is meant for learned as well as others, having two chapters dealing with scholastic philosophy and natural religion. It was thought out whilst the saint was on retreat at Mount Alverno, in the thirty-third year after the death of St. Francis.

It opens with a Prologue in which the writer reminds us that in our journey to God we must use both our natural and our supernatural powers, and then emphasizes the old truth that we come to the Father only by way of Jesus crucified. As no one attains to wisdom without grace, justice and knowledge, so no one reaches contemplation save by way of meditation and seeking for God, holy 'conversation' and devout prayer. 'Lest, perhaps, he might think it enough to have reading without unction, speculation without devotion, investigation without admiration, ... industry without piety, knowledge without charity, intellectual keenness without humility, study without grace, brilliance without wisdom divinely inspired.' The Saint addresses himself to 'those humble and pious souls who are prevented by divine grace, contrite and devout, anointed with the oil of divine joy, of lovers wisdom and on fire with longing, willing to be still and magnify God, love Him and savour Him.'

He then considers God in His universe, and all the visible world, and this ascent by steps is symbolized by the six wings of the Seraph which appeared to Francis.

---

[22] See R. P. Longpré, O. F. M., article: 'Bonaventure' in the *Dictionnaire de Spiritualité*.

No acquired knowledge can enable a man to enter into himself so that he may be interiorly delighted in the Lord, unless He intervenes who is 'the door', and we approach this door only if we believe in Him, hope in Him and love Him. If we would enter again as into Paradise, it can only be by means of the faith, hope and charity of the Mediator between God and man, who is the tree of life in the midst of Paradise.

The scholastic theologian speaks in the next chapter, and we have the nature of God set before us: a Being whose essence is His existence; absolutely simple without potentiality; most perfect; eternal; First Cause of all things, which exist only for Him; *Actus purus*. In this connection, he cites a definition which became a favourite with mediæval theologians: *God is an intelligible sphere, the centre of which is everywhere and the circumference nowhere.*[23] He reminds us also that 'the Scholastic of the East', St. John Damascene, tells us that the proper name of God is *Qui est*—He who is—and that Denys says His first name is *Bonum.*[24] Goodness is diffusive of itself, therefore the highest Goodness must be most diffusive of itself, and is so by means of generation and spiration. So we have the marvel of the Blessed Trinity, which is incomprehensible to us. We may contemplate God in three ways: outside of us, in His creation; within ourselves, by meditating upon His divine indwelling and working in us; and above ourselves by intellectual contemplation. Faith is the foundation of this last, for on earth even the highest forms of illumination are in the order of faith.[25] We are further warned that this light of God may be such that we seem in darkness, because we cannot bear its effulgence. Such contemplation will lead to ecstasy, but there still

---

[23] From Alanus de Insulis, *Theologiæ Regulæ*, P. L., CCX, col. 627. Cistercian, b. at Lille c. 1128, d. at Cîteaux c. 1203. He studied and taught at Paris and enjoyed a great reputation. A disciple of Augustine, he was also a follower of Plato, and influenced by Eriugena.
[24] *De fide orthodox.*, l. I, c. 12. *De divin. Nom.*, c. 6.
[25] *Coll. in Hex.*, III and VIII.

remains the contemplation of which the gift of wisdom is the formal principle, and there the soul can help only removing obstacles.[26]

The soul must forsake all that is not God, and especially itself; it must also leave sensible images, for God is above all these.[27] It must abandon itself to love and grace, for it is there we find the formal element of beatitude, and only the Holy Spirit can help here. There remains only ecstasy and rapture. The union thus obtained is one of ecstatic love;[28] contact with God is immediate in the ecstasy of this last stage, and there is none higher on earth. Nevertheless, it is not the union we shall know in the Beatific Vision. The two kinds of contemplation fuse, as the colours of the spectrum become just white! 'When our soul has been filled with the lights of Understanding, divine Wisdom dwells therein as in the house of God, and the soul becomes the daughter, bride and friend of God; a member and co-heir of Christ, the Head, and the temple of the Holy Spirit. It is grounded in faith, raised up by hope, and dedicated to God by sanctity of soul and body.'[29]

A modern Carthusian has expressed the same teaching in striking words:

> Love and faith will enlighten each other reciprocally. We shall go from light to light ... and each new light will engender a new motion of love. The effect of the union with God and the return of the powers of the soul to unity is, therefore, the simplification of the will and the understanding, and thereby their perfection; for the immaterial order, 'simple' means perfect. The spiritual life, properly so-called, follows the same line of progress.... 'Devotions', in which the powers of the soul are more or less dispersed, take on a single sense. Pious practices are gathered

---

[26] *Ibid.*, II. 28.
[27] St. John's teaching on this point is exactly the same.
[28] *Itin. ad Deum*, c. 4. *Coll in Hex. XXII.*
[29] *Ibid.*, c. 4.

together in one single act, *accepted* rather than produced, which is of immense price for it is of the divine order: it consists in letting God be in us. We may call it charity, faith, trust, adoration, propitiation, thanksgiving. Here, all words seem to become synonyms, and their concepts to fuse, like substances heated to melting point in the crucible of the heart wherein love itself is burning.[30]

The treatise *De septem donis Spiritus Sancti*—on the seven Gifts of the Holy Ghost—has the same teaching on contemplation, according as the gifts of Understanding or Wisdom predominate, and there is no need to repeat it, but whereas elsewhere the saint follows St. Augustine, in this work there are points of contact with Greek theories.[31] In speaking of 'beatitude', which here is synonymous with the Sapiential contemplation, he tells us that this sight, or 'vision' whereby we attain to God, and which is a foretaste of the intuitive vision of heaven, is not an intuition but rather a contuition; that is to say, the apprehension of the presence of the cause in a perceived effect. The uncreated light becomes the object of our knowledge, inasmuch as it is the cause of the created light which alone we perceive directly.[32]

By the enlightening of the Holy Spirit, we are led back to true knowledge, burning love and intense and enlightening faith, and thence to union with God. For this union is the end of the Giver of light, that thereby we may be led back to the 'deifying'—*deificam*—simplicity and perfect union with the Father. To this, which comes from Denys, Bonaventure adds some comments from Robert Grosseteste's commentary upon the latter. At first we are

---

[30] See *Un Chartreux parle*; from *Le Paradis blanc*, by Pierre van der Meer de Walcheren. The speaker was a Dutch monk in the charterhouse of Valsainte, near Gruyère. (Desclée de Brouwer, Paris.)
[31] See *Le Saint Esprit et ses dons selon S. Bonaventure*, by Fr. Bonnefoy, O. F. M., Études de *philosophie médiévale*, t. 10. (Paris, Vrin, 1929.)
[32] *Op. cit.*

distracted and divided by love of many and various things, and as a result of our very distractions we are narrowed and constrained; but simplicity is 'deifying' because the soul clings to God alone, who unites it to Himself, and makes it 'deiform', not substantially but by participation.

He proceeds to treat of grace, which is as a light having many rays, or degrees, of different virtues and spiritual adornments; for in that same grace *gratum faciens*[33] is given the Holy Spirit, which perfects the soul so that it may become the daughter of the Eternal Father, the bride of Christ and the temple of the same Holy Spirit. Hence that grace is appropriately called *gratum faciens*, since without it no one can merit, or advance in the things of God, or attain to eternal life.

Then follow the theological virtues, the Beatitudes and the fruits of the Spirit. By the first, we are carried to God and more immediately united to Him; Faith seeks and searches into God; Hope 'tastes' Him, and strengthens the soul against temptation; Charity holds God and embraces Him.

The whole theme of the book is: *Every best gift and every perfect gift is from above.*[34] Each gift is treated separately, the work is strictly traditional and full of quotations, which amaze one as showing the enormous amount of reading St. Bonaventure managed to put in amidst his multiple occupations. There is nothing very original, but it is a *précis* of all that the greatest patristic and mediæval theologians have taught on the subject. It has been strongly influenced by the *Moralia* of St. Gregory. Each gift 'holds a feast in its day' and each day has its morning, its noontide and its eventide. The morning corresponds to the Purgative Way, and the gift of Fear is treated at some length 'because it is the beginning of wisdom', which latter is the last and highest of the contemplative gifts. Fear is at first servile, but as the soul progresses it becomes the filial fear which

---

[33] Grace that makes the soul pleasing to God.
[34] James 1:17.

must be present throughout the spiritual life; by Piety, we acquire a tender, filial attitude towards God; and gradually the soul directs all its works to Him, so worshipping Him, whilst its love for its neighbour is purified and ennobled, in that it loves him for God's sake. With the dawning of Knowledge, the soul searches after and learns all truth. It learns Holy Scripture, and it also comes to know the world as it really is: its hollowness, its transitoriness, etc., whilst from creation it rises to the Creator. Fortitude first rectifies the concupiscences, and then guards the 'acts' of the soul: memory, intellect and will, finally subjecting those powers to the Blessed Trinity.

With Counsel, we come to the Illuminative Way. It is described as 'a passionate longing, directed by reason, to enquire concerning those things which ought or ought not to be done.'[35] In the morning, the soul arises to conform itself to the divine Will, as the Holy Spirit inspires, and it avoids all wilful sin. At noon, understanding and affections are informed by truth and charity, and seek earnestly to observe all the precepts of Our Lord; and at eventide it is inclined to seek and follow the Counsels of perfection, and here Bonaventure speaks at length on the divine indwelling of the Trinity. When the soul has thus resolved upon perfect living, all the powers are perfected and the banquet follows.

The last two gifts belong to the contemplative and unitive life. At noon, the soul dies to the world and can 'see God', and its prayer is that of mystical contemplation, and at eventide its labours are over; it rests in the Sabbath of the prayer of union. All wilful sins and imperfections have disappeared *but compunction remains*, and the beauty of this state is well described. 'The whole soul is aflame with the fire of compunction.' We are dealing with the 'classic' spirituality, which especially marks the old religious Orders, and with that peaceful, abiding sorrow for sin which is so grand and strong a thing. As Bonaventure

---

[35] John Damascene, *De fide orthod.*, l. 1, c. 22.

says: 'On the altar of love all is burnt', and in the words
of a great English preacher: 'Our very sins become merely
so much dry wood for the fire of love to consume.'[36]
The soul becomes deiform so far as may be. The day
knows no evening, for that life has begun which will be
perfected in heaven.

The last of Bonaventure's great mystical treatises is the
Illuminationes Ecclesiæ in Hexæmeron: a series of twenty-three
sermons in which the theme of the creation in seven days
is applied to the life of the Church and the individual
soul. The exemplarism, which marks all of Bonaventure's
theology, is very strikingly brought out: the Church in
heaven is the pattern for the Church Militant, as for the
individual; the hierarchy of the angels and the Blessed is
the model for the earthly hierarchy, and all the powers of
the soul must be ordered hierarchically likewise. It is not
an easy book to read, for its many divisions, sub-divisions
and minor sub-divisions can become bewildering, and
make it hard to keep hold of the thread of the reasoning.
This has long been recognized, and it has been suggested
that these sermons are a synopsis written out from memory, and some time later, by one or more of the saint's
disciples. This is suggested not only by many repetitions,
a tendency to return to a subject apparently concluded
some time previously, and other signs that someone has
been compiling, using the notes of more than one person,
but also by curious phrases in the third person: 'he says',
'he adds', without any indication as to who the 'he' is!

Like all Bonaventure's works, it abounds in quotations,
and repeats the teaching we have already had elsewhere.
The writer treats of the theological virtues, the gifts of
the Holy Ghost, the understanding of the Scriptures, the
Church and finally of high contemplation, and, again like
all his works, it is always Christocentric. He urges again
the need for complete detachment if a soul would progress
in prayer, and uses a gracious metaphor: 'The sculptor

---

removes material, he does not add anything; nevertheless, he leaves a most noble form.'

As usual, there is little about the lower stages, but we are told that 'souls not raised to contemplation are in winter; those raised to "mediocre" contemplation are in spring; those raised to ecstasy are in summer, and they will receive the autumn fruits.' By the 'spring' contemplation, possibly acquired contemplation is meant, for as we have seen, ecstasy need not mean anything more than intense infused contemplation. St. Bonaventure was Augustinian, and may well use the word with Augustine's definition in mind.

We are told, however, that this summer sun blinds when surely it ought rather to enlighten. 'But this blinding is the highest enlightening, for it is in the highest point of the soul, beyond the investigation of the human intellect. Therefore, there is an inaccessible cloud, which yet enlightens minds which have been lost amid such investigations. And this is what is meant when the Lord is said to dwell in a cloud, and to have made darkness His hiding place.[37] From this sun shine triple rays, like *lamps of fire*,[38] and this is the whole cause of the enkindling of contemplation, for the ray of glory never comes without enkindling as well as enlightening. When the soul is thus united to God, in one sense it sleeps, and in another it is wide awake. *I sleep, but my heart watches.*' Only the affective part of the soul watches and imposes silence upon all the other powers, and then the man is alienated from his senses, rapt into

---

[37] Surely, the anonymous author of the English mystical work, *The Cloud of Unknowing*, had read this book of St. Bonaventure!

[38] It seems obvious that St. John of the Cross borrowed also from the same source.

> 'And O, ye lamps of fire,
> In whose resplendent light
> The deepest caverns where the senses meet,
> Erst steeped in darkness dire,
> Blaze with new glories bright
> And to the lov'd one give both light and heat.'

ecstasy and hears words not given to man to utter, which are only in the affections. For they cannot be expressed save by one who has received them. This makes the soul as like to God as can be in this life. It has not glory as a *habit*, but it has it as an act.

The two works *Lignum vitæ* and *Vitis mystica* contain nothing fresh in one sense, but as we know that the former, in particular, was popular at the time of Carmelite reform, and the latter, being then ascribed to St. Bernard,[39] must also have been well known, they cannot be wholly omitted. The former is a devout treatise on the life of Our Lord, cast in the form of short paragraphs, obviously intended for use in meditation. As the longest can be read in about three minutes, it is clear that, among the Franciscans as among the Carmelites, the religious were not meant to spend much time in mere reading, but to pass forthwith to prayerful pondering on the mystery suggested. Here it is worthwhile to make a few remarks upon the devotion to the Sacred Humanity as practised in the Middle Ages proper, and with which the Franciscans are so especially associated—although St. Bernard might be hailed as the real pioneer—and the same devotion as it developed in the post-Reformation period, even among reformed Franciscan bodies such as the Capuchins. The former is tender, but not sentimental, far less verging upon the morbid. True, sometimes it goes into some detail, but it is never crudely realistic; above all, it is ever marked by the 'grievous joy' not found so often in sadder days. Devotion to the Sacred Heart was coming in,[40] but never in Bonaventure or his brethren do we

---

[39] There are several quotations from the *Lignum Vitæ* in the *Third Spiritual Alphabet* of the Franciscan, Fray Francisco de Osuna, one of the greatest mystical writers in Spain previous to St. John. He cites the last paragraph of the Preface, and there are citations from other works of Bonaventure. (See in particular chapters 6 and 21 of Osuna's book.)

[40] From the *Lignum Vitæ* is taken the first lesson of the third Nocturn of Matins for the feast of the Sacred Heart. The other

find any suggestion that the Sacred Heart is mourning over Its failures! They were too theological to let their emotions get the better of them. There can be no failure in the work of the Son of God! The men of the ages of faith loved to synthesize, and they never forgot Easter Day as they sorrowed over Good Friday. Christ crowned with thorns, the Man of Sorrows, was ever *Christus Rex*. How Bonaventure loves the title!

This work, as also the *Vitis mystica*, lets us look into the sanctuary of the saint's inner life. Love of the Passion, of the Mass, of the Blessed Sacrament, are outstanding features of his spirituality, and devotion to the Sacred Heart is knit up with these. Hence in the final meditations they have their place. Church and sacraments come forth from the pierced side of Christ, as He sleeps the sleep of the dead upon the Cross, and the doctrine of the Mystical Body is prominent. Some readers, as they peruse the final meditations, will be reminded of Benson's *Christ in the Church*, as the Seraphic Doctor points out how the Church suffers in her turn as her Head suffered.

The treatise is intended 'to build up faith and kindle devotion'. It opens with Our Lord's divine generation, and mentions some Old Testament types. Then follows the Incarnation, and the whole of His life up to the Ascension; finally He is considered as Head of the Church, King, Judge, and our last End. The author concludes by urging all to pray for the gifts of the Holy Spirit, whom the Son promised to send us. The final prayer deserves quoting, despite its length:

> We pray, therefore, the most merciful Father, by Thee, His only-begotten Son, made Man, crucified and glorified for our sakes, to send upon us, out of His treasures, the Spirit of sevenfold grace which rested upon Thee in all His fullness:

---

lessons of the same Nocturn are from *Vitis mystica* (S. Bernardus, t. III; P. L., CLXXXIV) and a number of short phrases from both works are found scattered through that Office.

the spirit of Wisdom, whereby we may taste the
life-giving fruit of the Tree of Life, which is
Thyself; the Spirit of Understanding, whereby
the contuition of our minds may be enlightened;
the Spirit of Counsel, whereby we may follow in
thy footprints, and enter into the straight paths;
the Spirit of Fortitude, whereby we may render
powerless the assaults of our enemies; the Spirit
of Knowledge, whereby we may be filled with
the light of thy holy doctrine, so as to discern
good from evil; the Spirit of Piety, by which we
may be clothed with thy loving-kindness; the
Spirit of Fear, so that, forsaking all evil, we may
be made tranquil in the authority of thy divine
Majesty. For these things Thou hast willed us to
ask in the holy Prayer which Thou has taught us;
and these we seek now to obtain by thy Cross,
to the praise of thy Holy Name, to whom, with
the Father and the Holy Spirit, be all honour,
glory, thanksgiving, majesty and power, world
without end. Amen.

The work purports to be written for simple folk, and
contains moving exhortations to sinners to repent and
take courage, no matter what their past may have been.
It contains such prayers as the following: 'Look down, O
Lord, Holy Father, from Thy sanctuary, and Thy dwelling
in the highest heavens; look down, I say, upon the face
of Thy Christ! Look upon this most holy sacrifice which
our High Priest is offering to Thee for our sins, and be
appeased upon the wickedness of Thy people!' At the
close, he soars aloft into the heights of mystical prayer,
speaking as in other passages, and ends on the words:
'Let every tongue give thanks to Thee, O Father, for the
unspeakable gift of Thy overflowing charity, which hast
not spared the only Son of Thy heart, but hast delivered
Him to death for us all; that we might have so great and
so faithful an Advocate before Thee in heaven!'

Vitis Mystica presents some problems. As we have seen,
it was long fathered upon St. Bernard, but in the Latin

Patrology it is there acknowledged that it is not by him, but by 'some other pious author, who is neither unlearned nor inelegant.' Subsequent research has established the Bonaventuran authorship, though not of the whole book as it has come down to us. The original work was shorter, and the earlier portion is far the finer. In style and content it closely resembles the *Lignum Vitæ*, but soon after the section on the Crucifixion the former changes and becomes progressively less like that of the saint. Originally an almost passionate outpouring of love and adoration of Our Lord, it develops into a long treatise on the religious life, addressed to nuns, and is very 'ordinary' in content, sentimental in places and overburdened with figures of speech. The familiar similes of the rose, the lily and the violet, symbolizing love, purity and humility, are artificially worked to death!

The work has been described as a sermon and, certainly, in the short preface the writer does pray for himself as 'a humble minister', and asks that eternal life may be granted 'to the speaker and the hearers.' The earlier portion may have formed one or more public discourses, but it is difficult to decide concerning the more than a score of later chapters. Nor is it easy to decide where the break comes. The portion on the Crucifixion is soon followed by the words: 'Let us come to the end,'[41] and thenceforth the style deteriorates, although the new portion up to the sixteenth chapter is still better than what follows. It is possible that more than one later writer has worked over it.

The genuine work has an alternative title, *Treatise on the Passion of the Lord*, but whatever it may be called, the earlier part is a prolonged prayer, an outpouring of a loving soul. It opens thus: 'O gracious Jesus, true vine, tree of life, standing in the midst of Paradise!'[42] and is full of devotion to the Sacred Heart, as also of teaching on the Mystical Body. The thirteenth century, during which the

---

[41] *Vitis Mystica*, c. IV.
[42] '*O Jesus benigne, vitis vera, Lignum vitæ, quod in medio Paradisi situm est!*'

theology of the Holy Ghost was being worked out, saw also the doctrine of the Mystical Body come to the fore. 'Christ and the Church are one vine', writes Bonaventure, 'and so one body.' We find it notably in St. Thomas,[43] but St. Bonaventure runs him close. In this work, also, there are passages on the Blessed Sacrament, the author emphasizing the truth that although Christ is our food, He is not assimilated into us but we into Him.[44] In the fifth chapter we find the passage 'The whole life of Christ was a cross and martyrdom'—*Tota vita Christi crux fuit et martyrium*—familiar to all readers of the *Imitation*, inserted by the author of the latter work in the famous chapter, '*Of the King's highway of the Holy Cross*'.[45] Besides the portion of the Office of the Sacred Heart to which we have alluded, several phrases, here and there, from *Vitis Mystica* have found their way into the liturgy for that feast.[46]

A last sample of the style of the work may end our considerations:

> I have found the Heart of the King, the Brother, the loving Friend, Jesus. For I may say boldly that His Heart is mine, since my Head is Christ. How shall what is my head not be mine? And

---

[43] *Summa Theol.*, III, qq. 48–49, 62 and 69. *De verit.*, q. 2, art. 7; III *Sent.*, d. 18, q. 1, art. 6; In *Epist. Coll.*, I, 24, lect. 6: (2).

[44] *Vitis Mystica*, c. 4.

[45] *Imit.*, B. II, c. 12. In the *Alphabetum Religiosorum*, a short collection of pithy sentences arranged in alphabetical order, which though not by Bonaventure may contain sentences of his, and is certainly in accord with his teaching to his friars, we find another sentence from the *Imitation: Ama nesciri et pro nihilo reputari* (B. I, c. 2), 'Love to be unknown and esteemed as nought', since other well-known spiritual works of the period of the *Devotio moderna* are now proved to be less original than was formerly believed, it would be interesting to know how much of this great spiritual classic was borrowed from earlier writers.

[46] In particular we have the prayer: *Admitte tantum preces meas in sacrarium exauditionis*. These words also occur in the Proper Office for *Our Lady of Consolation*, the titular feast of the writer's own monastery, and with the substitution of *sanctuarium for sacrarium*— probably a 'slip' when citing from memory—they were frequently on the lips and the pen of the late Abbot Marmion.

shall I not adore? Therefore since I have found thy Heart and mine, O tender Jesus, I will pray Thee, my God: Only admit my prayers into the sanctuary where all prayers are heard; yes, draw me wholly into thy Heart!

There remains one short work to be noticed, before we turn to those which directly concern religious life and are ascetic rather than mystical. The *Soliloquy* is literally a soliloquy and, to be honest, a piece of plagiarizing, for it is a dialogue between *Homo* and *Anima* exactly on the lines of the Betrothal Gift of Hugh of St. Victor. In one edition of the saint's works, it is described as 'full of devotion rather than erudition'. It is, however, directly concerned with the interior life, and is very practical. It consists of four chapters. It opens with the text from Ephesians: *For this cause I bow my knees to the Father of Our Lord Jesus Christ . . . that you may know the length and breadth and depth and height etc.*[47]

Anima asks how it may attain to this, and *Homo* replies that the beginning is self-knowledge. The soul suffers at the sight of its sins, and is exhorted to trust in God's mercy. It must now turn to 'contemplation' which here is equivalent to meditation, and the Purgative Way takes up the greater portion of the book. The self-examination of *Anima* is very thorough, and it suffers acutely at the discoveries made, but *Homo* is encouraging, and assures it that it is beginning well and bids it pray to Our Lord, and betake itself now to consideration of the Passion. It now suffers much from dryness, and feels no consolation at all, and asks why this is so; *Homo* replies: 'I think it is because you wished to share His consolations before you had shared His Passion; to partake of His reward before imitating His virtues.' *Anima* is then told to think on the Four Last Things, and obeys, but asks what is the use of 'this lamentable meditation'. Then *Homo*, having explained the need of such meditation, allows the poor soul

---

[47] Eph. 3:14-19.

to meditate upon heaven and future beatitude; but when the latter asks how it is that in heaven the body will help the soul, but here on earth it proves an obstacle to the soul's contemplation, and drags it down: *Homo* dismisses the question as *scrupulosa*, and showing 'more curiosity than devotion'. In heaven our mode of understanding will be different, and the body will be a glorified one. *Anima* finally acknowledges the benefit it has obtained from the teaching of *Homo*.

May it be said that *Homo* sounds at times rather priggish, and one feels sympathy for *Anima?* The work is full of quotations and inferior to Hugh's *De arrha animæ*, but it has a value as teaching more at length of the middle stage of the spiritual life, and explaining more clearly the Night of the Senses than any other work of St. Bonaventure. There is also a good description of the later Night, when he deals with the soul's longing for God, its deep sense of its unworthiness, its helplessness, the long aridity, the monotony, that walking in darkness by faith, possible only because the soul believes in a dawn. It seems very likely that St. John of the Cross had studied this work.

There remain two books written by the saint which deal specifically with the religious life, and only incidentally with anything mystical, properly so called. It is impossible to go into detail here, though one in particular would repay complete translation; it can scarcely be doubted that they were read by the first Carmelites for they contain admirable teaching for all religious. The longer treatise: *De sex Alis Seraphim*—the Six wings of the Seraphim—as its title suggests, retains the prevailing style of symbol and simile, each wing standing for a different virtue, but one soon forgets everything but the shrewdness, the extraordinary insight into human nature, and surely, the unsurpassed knowledge of life in a religious house which the author exhibits. It deals with every facet of the life, and is especially concerned with Superiors. One realizes that the writer must have made many canonical visitations, and that he speaks from first-hand knowledge and experience. He frequently quotes the Rule of St. Benedict verbatim, and occasionally also that of St. Augustine. Only the merest sketch is possible here.

'There is a great difference in knowing how to live humbly below another, peacefully on a level with him, and profitably when presiding over him.' Some religious are content with 'good mediocrity'. As community men, they have been good, but as Superiors such will be pernicious; for since they lack spiritual ambition themselves, they will not foster it in others, neither are they equipped to help those who need help, especially the young, the weak and the troubled.

Of course some religious can do without such help, but they must have certain qualities: they must be fervent in 'devotion'—here meant in the Thomist sense; persons whose sense of duty makes them prompt to do whatever they think God requires of them. They must really love Him, and 'as it were naturally' have an abiding horror of sin. They must be able to live peacefully and quietly with their Brethren, not be puffed up because of their good observance, nor consider themselves faultless, and they must be stable characters who know themselves. Such are rare; 'few can live without a yoke' and even the Superior must not think himself dispensed from taking advice; even the Pope allows himself to be advised and guided by others.

'Good' religious fall into three categories: those who do no evil certainly, but neither do they do much good. They are negative, and 'live like baptized children'. The second category is rather better. They are more positive, 'instant in prayer', energetic in good works; but though they neglect nothing, they are not spiritually ambitious; they do not strive after holiness. They are content to say their Office, make the private prayer laid down by Rule, fast, labour as required of them, but they leave higher standards to others. They are satisfied with a blameless

and pious routine, but as for envisaging the possibility
of sanctity—preposterous! The third kind are those who
take as seriously as possible the obligations and implica-
tions of their Profession. They desire familiar friendship
with God and are prepared to pay the price; for lesser
spiritual or temporal consolations they care not. They
are not always burning with zeal against others' sins and
failings, though they want all to be holy. If such becomes
Superiors, however, they may have one fault: namely a
tendency to guard their own peace too zealously, and so
fail in correcting and training their subjects, thus allowing
abuses to creep in.

Anon, Bonaventure turns to Superiors, and lays it down
that a good Superior makes a good community. He lays
down also both the divine and ecclesiastical law, the obligations of religious life, etc. Transgression of the lesser
matters of the life 'deforms the beauty of religion, hinders
spiritual progress and disedifies others'. But here the
Superior must be wide-minded, and not unduly magnify
trifles. Some Superiors penance an omitted genuflexion in
choir more severely than a case of detraction; are more
indignant over a versicle, or a small rubric—*rubricula*—
than over some serious upset in the house which causes
scandal. Above all, the Superior must be a man of prayer,
otherwise all his works will be sterile: 'The structure of
good works which is not held together by frequent and
devout prayer is like a stone wall without mortar.'

Nevertheless, he must draw the line between zeal and
fussy scrupulosity; he must maintain discipline, and never
allow himself to be overpersuaded or pestered into giving
in by someone's importunity or clever manœuvring; and
there are two kinds of people whose advice no prudent
man should take: sycophants and flatterers!

He must guard against abusing his authority and not
pervert it to minister to his own honour or convenience;
and he must remember that he will have to give account
for all the sins of his subjects which he has not tried to

correct. He must remember that he is a Father and the community is a family, and a good family spirit must be fostered. He must not neglect his religious for any outside interests, however important he may think these latter, and he must aim at knowing all individually and dealing with them accordingly. He ends with some understanding advice to the Superior as to the safe-guarding of his own spiritual life.

The other work was written for Isabel de Valois, the royal Poor Clare[48] and her nuns, and is known as *De Perfectione Vitæ ad Sorores* and also *De Perfectione Animæ*. It consists of eight chapters. It follows directly along the lines of the *De triplici via* and is much less original than the work we have just been considering. Quotations are many, and familiar to us, and naturally, in a work from Franciscans ruled by a king's daughter, the saint insists much on holy Poverty. The fifth chapter, dealing with prayer, is the most relevant for our purpose, the rest being concerned with the classic religious virtues to be sought in any community. Prayer 'is a virtue of such efficacy that of itself it can completely subdue all the cunning devices of its implacable foe, the devil. . . . There is then no cause for surprise that the religious who is not devoted to the practice of prayer frequently succumbs to temptation.' All our sins are due to negligence, concupiscence—really self-love in its widest sense—or malice; and under these three heads the nun must examine herself. She must watch against neglect of prayer, reading and manual work, and against vanity, immortification and *acedia*. Again, Bonaventure insists upon the danger of this last for, thanks to

---

[48] Blessed Isabel de Valois was the favourite sister of St. Louis. She was born in 1225 and died in 1270. Having resolved to be a religious, she learnt Latin in order to be able to read the Vulgate and the Fathers, and subsequently founded the Monastery of Longchamps. The Rule, drawn up by some Franciscans in France, was a mitigation of that of St. Clare, and was confirmed by Urban IV in 1263; hence the name 'Urbanists' given to those religious who followed it.

it, the religious becomes lukewarm, dreamy, undevout at
Mass and Office, talkative, idle, unpunctual and looking
miserable!

Perhaps also because he is writing for religious, who
could in all probability read his other books, the author
says little of the earlier stages of prayer, and passes almost
at once to contemplation treated, as always, in both its
forms, intellectual and 'Sapiential', but he does insist
strongly upon the debt of honour under which religious
lie to aim at real holiness. It does not befit a soul fash-
ioned to the divine image, and stamped with the likeness
of God, to fritter away its time with earthly cares. 'A soul
redeemed with Christ's most precious blood, and created
for eternal happiness, ought to rise even above the angels
and the cherubim; it ought to ascend and contemplate
the Most Holy Trinity.'

IV

THE PSEUDO-BONAVENTURE

I. FRANCISCAN WRITERS

SEVERAL WORKS DEALING WITH THE training of novices were assigned to St. Bonaventure, but none are by him though all are in accord with his teaching. The *Speculum Discipline ad Novitios* is by Bernard of Bessa, his disciple and secretary, who knew him intimately, and is still in use in modern Franciscan novitiates. It is an excellent piece of work and follows strictly traditional lines, not the least interesting feature being its close kinship with similar writings by members of other Orders, showing how all see alike on the most important matters. It contains a number of quotations from the Benedictine Rule and from St. Bernard, but the most interesting items are obviously the fruit of the writer's experience.

There is less corporal penance prescribed than formerly, but emphasis is laid upon careful individual training, and the latter is less vague than hitherto. For example, the novices are to go to confession three times in the week, and not to change their confessor. Novice-masters and Superiors generally are to show 'the gentleness of a mother' as well as the austerity of a father; frivolity and levity, however, are to be corrected, and novices are not to laugh when reprimanded! There is much insistence upon private prayer, but for young people Fr. Bernard prefers shorter and more frequent periods, rather than fewer and longer ones. His instructions upon the Divine Office, its importance and fitting performance, yield in nothing to those of St. Benedict, and he is particular in requiring that when said in private—as Franciscans will often have to do when out preaching—care must be taken that it is recited reverently and recollectedly.

The twentieth chapter is concerned with the young professed, and is very wise. Such must be careful once they have left the noviciate lest, freed from the watchful care and candid tongue of their Master, they relax; and they must remember that small faults lead to greater ones. Let them beware of omitting their mental prayer, or regular confession, and let them never forget that conceit and self-complacency are temptations to young religious, especially should these be put into office. 'Three things become any religious whomsoever: to speak little, to be familiar with few, and to pray much.'

The *De profectu religiosorum*—Of the setting out upon the religious life—is by David of Augsburg, being a synthesis of three of his works. He was Master of Novices at the friary of Ratisbon in the early thirteenth century, and died at Augsburg in 1272. Up to the death of St. John of the Cross, like the other works of this class, it was assigned to St. Bonaventure himself, and it shows the same sound psychology found in that saint's writings.

It opens with four *Cautions*—a word used in the same sense by St. John in a small work for his nuns at Beas— which are as follows: Strive never to lose the first fervour of your noviciate; never let yourself be affected by bad example, and never argue: 'It is right for others, so why not for me?'; never judge others rashly; and never let yourself give way under trial and temptation.

There are three kinds of religious: those who shirk the hard things leading to sanctity, and are content to avoid grievous sin; those who practise great bodily austerity, but are censorious hard, and neglect the more important side of spiritual life altogether; and those who really set themselves to work at that thorough re-education of the inner and outer man, which is meant by 'conversion' or 'holy conversation', in the old traditional sense.

Above all, there is more helpful instruction upon prayer for beginners than we have found hitherto. Vocal prayers, apart from the Office, are necessary for such as have not yet 'the affection of devotion', otherwise they may waste their time and become lukewarm. Those, however, who 'have greater familiarity with God' and find such vocal prayer an obstacle, may take what helps them and leave the rest. These latter will cease to need words, but when they are less well disposed let them observe the good custom of vocal prayer. When God visits them with 'greater infusion of devotion' they can omit them altogether; Fr. David says there must be *cordis libertas*—liberty of spirit. There can be no uniform rule as to what prayers are best for individuals; different kinds of prayer suit different people, like different kinds of food! Whatever prayer a soul finds best raises it to God, is the best kind for that soul. All this instruction is exactly that of St. John of the Cross, and we here find clearly the lower, or acquired, contemplation.

The end of all prayer is to cling to God and become one spirit with Him, by means of the purest love and most peaceful knowledge; 'hidden in the shadow of His face from the clamour of earthly things, in the quiet of fruition, where all the soul's powers are gathered into one, and transformed into a certain likeness of the divine "conformation" and eternal stability'.

Certain similes and remarks of the author remind us at once of the great Spaniards: multiplicity of distractions and agitation of the extroverted soul die down with preserving efforts at recollection, and whereas at first one felt as when entering a dark room where it is impossible to see anything, gradually we begin to distinguish larger objects and finally everything. Visions and suchlike features are suspect and must never be credited without consulting a wise director, and the soul must guard against pride, least it be deceived by the devil masquerading as an angel of light. The kinds of visions, locutions, etc., are explained as by St. John, and another feature the two writers have in common is some definite instruction on the faults of devout persons, 'imperfect and new-comers' to contemplative life, as the Franciscan calls them. The treatise ends with some discussion on the subject of frequent Communion, and for its period the instruction is 'advanced'. Although the author considers weekly Communion sufficient for religious and devout folk in general, he is quite ready to allow those who so desire, and whose lives are edifying, to receive more frequently, and mentions that he has known souls to long for Holy Communion so intensely that their physical health was affected.

His description of the Unitive Way is beautiful, but he denies that any creature can ever love God as it is loved by Him; there can be likeness, but never 'equality', and here he would have differed from St. John,[1] at least apparently. In his treatment of ecstasy also, he rather departs from the earlier position, for he alludes to the body weakening under it. The body is shattered like a glass in the fire—the fire of the Holy Spirit.

We come now to the two most important works classed as 'Pseudo-Bonaventure': the *Stimulus Amoris* or *Goad of Love*, as it is known in English, and the *Mystical Theology*, which, however, is not by a Franciscan, so will be considered apart.

The former was ascribed to Bonaventure as late as 1869, when a new Latin edition appeared at Naples; and the book was translated into English in 1642 by a Franciscan of Douay, Lewis Augustine. A preface, encouraging the persecuted English Catholics, was added. Among the *Approbations*, corresponding to a modern *Nihil Obstat*, is one by Dom Rudesind Barlow, Superior of the English Benedictines at St. Gregory's Douay; a Doctor of Theology and brother of the Benedictine Marty, Blessed Ambrose Barlow.

The author is now known to have been Fr. James of Milan, and the date of publication towards the end of the thirteenth century. It has been called 'a masterpiece

---

[1] *Spirit. Cant.* (A), S. 37, n. 2.

of tender devotion to our suffering Lord', and strongly resembles the *Lignum Vitæ* and *Vitis Mystica*, although it contains some lapses from good taste.[2] It has three parts, of which the third is probably by another hand. The first is concerned wholly with the Passion, the second is ascetic and to some extent mystical, whilst the third is general, dealing with the contemplative life in ten chapters but afterwards becoming rather ordinary, with meditations on the *Pater, Ave, Salve Regina*, etc., inferior to the rest.

'To attain to the quiet of contemplation, three things are needful: firstly, the soul must realize the gravity of sin and have fervent contrition; secondly, it must then enter into the wound of Christ's side, and so into His Heart. Thirdly, the soul must desire to possess nothing but God', and we find the expression *solus Soli*—to be alone with Him who is alone—which is not seldom claimed as peculiarly Carmelite! The Discalced Carmelites may have loved it, but they did not invent it.

There is a suggestion of both St. John and St. Ignatius' *Third Degree* in one passage. 'Beholding His Lord condemned and insulted, the true contemplative doth now no more desire temporal honours, but longs with all his heart to suffer, and to endure with his Lord all injury, abjection and derision, by which he may, in some measure, be conformable to Him . . . and although he might equally and indifferently enjoy both, yet would rather choose to be dispraised than honoured.'[3] He has a passage on the sufferings of Our Lady, which is striking: 'The Mother knew that her Son was suffering for her, as for the rest of the redeemed', and he also connects the gifts of the Holy Ghost with the Passion. 'So this excellent contemplative, by the gift of Wisdom in the Passion of Christ, abstracting himself from all outward things, and tending wholly towards God, is raised above all things, and being

---

[2] See article by R. F. C. Fischer, O. F. M., in the *Dictionnaire de Théologie: Pseudo-Bonaventure*.

[3] Part I, c. 7.

separated from himself, his heart and meditation is con-
versant and busied only about the honour of God, and
the abasement and affliction of Christ.'[4]

In the second part of the work, the way of perfection is likened to climbing a mountain in the shortest
time possible. We have the metaphor which the Spanish
Franciscan, Bernardino de Laredo, will use in his *Ascent
of Mount Sion*, and St. John in his *Ascent of Mount Carmel*,
wherein he will urge taking the short way up, without
winding or compromise: *Nada! Nada! Nada!*[5] and that
because we are in haste. His teaching has nothing especially new about it. Meditation and affective prayer yield
place to another form, at first full of sweetness, but that,
in its turn, is replaced by yet another, wherein God 'hides
Himself again and again', in order to make us seek Him
more earnestly. This, the author calls 'darkness', but for
him it is not a constant condition, extending over a long
period, but rather a darkness that lifts and shuts down
again. This teaching may be based upon his own experience with souls, for it is not uncommon at the beginning
of the Illuminative Way. He speaks of the Transforming
union as do others, and we recognize Denys: 'Then does
the soul lift itself above itself. It enters into the divine
darkness; and there doth it cry out and say: *And the
night is my light in my delight.*'[6] But, remembering that he
is writing for those whose vocation is actively apostolic,
he reminds them that Martha and Mary are never to
be separated. 'When a man has become after a manner
deified and transformed into God, to whatsoever he turns
himself he will consider nothing but God ... he shall see
God in all things, and in his active labours shall enjoy
the contemplative life.'[7]

---

[4] *Ibid.*
[5] Nothing!
[6] Part II, c. 6. The version of Scripture quoted is that used by the
English translator at Douay (Ps. 138:11).
[7] Part II, c. 6.

2. HUGH OF BALMA

The authorship of the *Mystical Theology*, long erroneously ascribed to St. Bonaventure, has been a subject of controversy for centuries and still remains such. One elaborate theory after another has been put forward, only to be disproved by contrary evidence. It has been assigned to the Franciscan, Henry of Baume, sometime confessor to St. Colette; to a Carthusian, Henry of Balma, who does not seem every to have existed, to another monk of the same Order, Hugh of Palma, of whom, likewise, nothing certain seems known, and to the celebrated Henry of Kalkar, a distinguished member of the famous charter-house of Cologne, who greatly influenced the *Brethren of the Common Life*.[8] The latest research, however, makes it reasonably certain that it is the work of Hugh of Balma, or perhaps, Balmey, and this is supported by both internal and external evidence.[9] As found among Bonaventure's works, the *Prologue* contains a passage altered by some Franciscan from its original form. There, the reader is bidden to thank God for having called him into the Franciscan Order, which is under the special patronage of St. John the Baptist; but that saint is not the special patron of the Friars Minor, whereas he is of the Carthusians. These, on their side, relate, in the ordinary course of their history, that: 'About this time', seemingly 1295, 'flourished Hugh of Balma, author of the golden *De Triplici via*: Of the threefold way to Wisdom, namely, Purgative, Illuminative, and Unitive; which beings: *Viæ Sion lugent.*' Such are the

---

[8] He was born at Kalkar, near Cleves, 1328, studied at Paris, where he was both a professor, and Procurator for the German nation, and entered the monastery at Cologne in 1365. One of the reforming party at the time of the Great Schism, he was Superior in several houses of his Order, including two in the Low Countries, where he was a friend of the Windesheim Canons. He died at Cologne in 1365. He wrote several books, but only one was published: *The Book of Exercises of a Monk*, into which he incorporated portions of the *Mystical Theology*, including the Prologue.

[9] 4 See Vernet, *La spiritualité médiévale*.

opening words of this treatise, which, adds the Carthusian annalist, is known also as the *Mystica Theologia*.[10] It is a remarkable work and one Franciscan scholar writes that 'it marks a date in the history of speculative mysticism'.[11] Alas, that we do not know the date! It was well known in Spain, and the Spanish translation was made by the unfortunate Father Jerome Gracian; but Bernardino de Laredo quotes it frequently earlier, and, believing it to be by Henry of Baume, regards it as a Franciscan work.

This being so, it is tantalizing to know so little of the author. The Carthusian annalist merely states the fact of Hugh's authorship, and refers to the alteration made by the Franciscans, quoting the passage as in the Carthusian manuscripts, where the reader is urged to thank God for having called him to the *Carthusian* Order. Even the dates assigned to this elusive monk vary by many years. It is commonly held that Bonaventure's *De Triplici Via* and Hugh's treatise, which is often called by the same title, were written about the same time: hence the confusion. Hugh of Balma, or Balmey, is stated to have been Prior of the charterhouse of Méyriat, in the diocese of Lyons—later in that of Belley—which monastery had been founded in 1116, by one, Ponce de Balmey, a canon of Lyons who became a Carthusian, and others of the name are found in the Order at different dates.

In the early years of the present century, a French Jesuit scholar suggested a solution which, albeit already disproved, has led to further research among the Carthusians themselves which may yield results. He claimed to have proved from internal evidence that the author of the treatise was Henry of Kalkar, but that Hugh of Balma had copied it, assigning the latter to the early years of the fifteenth century. However, as Hugh of Balma is cited verbatim in a notable work, *De contemplatione*, by the Carthusian mystic Guigo du Pont, who died in 1297, some

---

[10] *Annales Ordinis Cartusiensis*, t. III, year 1205.
[11] R. F. Fischer, O. F. M., Dict. *de théologie: Psuedo-Bonaventure*.

years after his work appeared, it is obvious that Henry of Kalkar did the copying, and that the *Viæ Sion lugent*, evidently already sufficiently well known, cannot be later than the middle of the thirteenth century, at the latest.

The work is sometimes obscure, consisting of a Prologue, three chapters, dealing respectively with the three ways, and a discussion, called the *Quaestio unica*, at the end. It is evident that more than one hand has worked over the manuscript, and other Franciscan interpolations are found, obviously not at home in the original text.

The author follows Denys and differs markedly from St. Bonaventure when treating of contemplation, whilst using St. Bernard and the Victorines. He is original, and often draws upon his own experience in spiritual matters and his observation of others. He shows a definite distaste for over-much study for religious, and warns his readers that such as really desire to reach the highest union with God will not succeed by poring over Aristotle! He repeats that even the simplest people—'even layfolk'—can do what is required on the soul's part; though here he may refer to the lay brethren, who among the Carthusians were always very carefully trained.

He thus explains contemplation: the soul was created to be a seat of Wisdom, wherein the King of Peace—*Rex pacificus*—of the supernal city, God Almighty, might dwell. The study of how this comes about is called *Mystical Theology*. It was taught by St. Paul, then 'his disciple' Denys, who gathered up his teaching, and explained it in writing; it is an account of how the soul progresses towards God through the desire of love. God enlightens the soul so that it may find out certain things about Him: that He is the First Cause, the Creator, the source of all goodness and beatitude. The understanding being thus enlightened, the affections are aroused, so that eventually the soul rests in God without any intermediary. At first its love is imperfect, but by practising itself in many aspirations of love, it becomes increasingly purer, and a day will come when, 'more quickly than thought, it is uplifted by the Creator's right hand, without any previous thinking, as often as He pleases, even a hundred times a day or a night; so that by continually aspiring to Him, it becomes fixed in Him'. This union takes place in the apex of the soul, and there the soul finds experimentally the origin of all wisdom. This is the work of the Holy Spirit, and though the soul can help itself at the earlier stage, it cannot of itself rise to this union with God; nor can reason understand or understanding speculate upon it. It is a matter of: *Taste and see how sweet the Lord is!*

The author now begins at the beginning, and says something new and rather surprising. The soul in earnest 'may enter upon the Purgative way in a month or two, according as God sees fit to shed His divine light upon it, more or less quickly'. A little later on, he gives the usual waring as to the trials the soul must expect, and encourages it to persevere under them. Now St. John of the Cross teaches that the *Night of the Senses*, that aridity characteristic of the transition from the Purgative to the Illuminative Way, and from meditation to the 'beginners' contemplation'—'acquired contemplation' to the Carmelites—usually sets in not long after the soul's first conversion, and that the majority of earnest souls enter this stage.[12] He teaches that his spiritual phenomenon marks the end of the Purgative Way, but of course there can be no hard and fast frontier line. The change sets in gradually; for a longer or shorter while, the soul may sometimes be able to resume its former meditation and affective prayer with the old facility; but sooner or later this becomes impossible, and it is left, like Sir Percivale, 'alone and thirsting, in a land of sand and thorns'. There seems little, if any, doubt that Hugh of Balma and John of the Cross refer to the same thing and have made the same discovery from practical direction of souls.

---

[12] *Dark Night*, B. I, c. 8, n. 4.

As says St. Bernard, the soul must approach its Lord by kissing first His foot, then His hand and lastly His lips.[13] It does the first by thinking upon its sins, the second by considering His goodness to us and the third by clinging to Him alone by means of burning affection. By means of the exercises proper to the Illuminative Way, it will rise still higher, and gain an experimental knowledge of God, who inwardly teaches it what no mortal effort or eloquence can do. Neither Plato nor Aristotle, nor any human philosophy, or science, can understand what God alone teaches the soul; and every rational soul may learn from the highest of all teachers a knowledge before which all human reason and understanding fails. This, again, is *Mystical Theology*.

We now come to details and note wide liberty of spirit. True, the soul begins by meditating on its sins, but perfect freedom is allowed as regards acts and aspirations, and though the author does suggest examples, he bids his readers use these only if they are found helpful. The soul should turn its thoughts to God, His nature, attributes, benefits, etc., and thus humbled, it is moved to ask the pardon for which it may confidently hope. It must then meditate on the love of God, and pray for others; for it must imitate Him who sends His rain upon the just and the unjust. All men have been created to the image of the Blessed Trinity, and all redeemed by Christ; consequently, we must pray for mercy upon all without exception. Especially must we pray that all may come to know the truth. The soul should often turn to Our Lady for help, and greet her with an *Ave*, during the day, and to act thus is better than to pray before a picture or statue of her. Of course the soul must work ascetically at itself. The rays of the spiritual, as of the material, sun cannot penetrate a room unless the windows are clean. God, our Sun, is only waiting for that to flood the soul with His light. And let that soul know that, provided it is ready to kiss the foot and hand, there is no presumption

---

[13] *Serm. in Cant.*, III.

whatever in aspiring to intimate union with God: the kiss
of the mouth. But it must be prepared to labour and suffer.
Farmers toil, and put up with bad weather, failure of crops
and losses; merchants take risks, such as the loss of their
ships and cargoes at sea; surely, if these endure all, and
work for temporal gain, a soul stamped with the image
of the Trinity should do likewise, and above all a religious
who has solemnly bound himself to God!

Prayer is the bread of the soul, and as the body cannot
live without food, so the soul will die without prayer. It
must be faithful to its prayer, and keep to fixed times
and places. 'Whether he be hot or cold, whether he feel
devotion or no, let him watch at the gate of God's tender
mercy, and he will be aware of that Beloved who created
him to His own image. Let him not desist, but go on
knocking, until he hear his Beloved sweetly consoling
him in the quiet voice of love.'

Having gained self-knowledge, and been seriously con-
verted, the soul should meditate upon the life and Passion
of Our Lord, Holy Scripture, etc., but the author recognizes that dryness may continue, and again we have: 'Let
him be content with the crumbs;' but he must persevere
and 'desire crumbs, not ardour'. All this suffering and
'wearing down'—*attritiones*—is getting rid of sinfulness and
imperfection, and we must remember that this passive
purification is much more effective than the active work
the soul is doing by battling with its lower nature.

By now, it is in the Illuminative Way, but its prayer
is not yet passive, save occasionally. It must help itself,
no longer by elaborate meditation, but by simple pondering upon some truth, and loving aspirations; and as
an example of what he means, the author, like St. Teresa
at a later day, suggests simply taking the Lord's Prayer,
sentence by sentence:

Our Father: 'God begets many children by the seed of
deifying love.' 'Then shall I be thy true child, when I
embrace Thee, clasping Thee to me with true love.' 'Oh

when shall I love Thee? When shall I love Thee so ardently that a little of Thy loving-kindness may be seen in me?'

Hallowed be thy name: 'O when shall I hold Thee? For earth will have no place in me when Thou, O loving Father, dwellest in me by Thy grace and Thy love.'

Thy kingdom come: 'God's kingdom comes in the soul when, so far as is compatible with earthly weakness, its will is completely given to Him. But He cannot reign in a soul until all vain-glory and selfishness have been driven out.'

Our daily bread: This means frequent Holy Communion, and grace to be faithful to prayer, which, as has been said, is the 'bread and wine' of the soul. Thus is love nourished, and without love there can be no union with God.

This day: Today means our present life, but eternity is simple and one, and the love of eternity is begun in our earthly life. 'That love wherewith the Bridegroom is loved in this life is one with the love wherewith in the eternity of glory, the soul will be united to the Ruler of all.'

Forgive us our trespasses: We must ask here to be freed from all venial sin, for mortal sin should now be unthinkable.

At the end of the *Pater noster* is a petition that the soul may not go to purgatory, but be purified in this life; not to escape suffering, but because it so longs to see God, and since the fire of love is more effective than that of purgatory, it prays that love may burn away its stains.

Soon, the soul will find that it needs not even the most simplified meditation, and as soon as it goes to prayer it will be united to God. After all, the object of meditation, etc., was only to kindle affection! It is like the wooden scaffolding men erect when they want to build a stone bridge. When the stone is firmly fixed in position, you can remove the scaffolding. 'And so, by means of previous meditation, by these aspirations, little by little, the affections are enkindled, and as the tow[14] when exposed

---

[14] *Stuppa* means a tow wick dipped in some inflammable mixture.

to the sun's rays, dries up, and at once bursts into flame,
so love is increasingly enkindled in the soul, until the
latter is raised to the Unitive state.'

'But, O most loving Lord, how shall I come to be one
mind with Thee, save only by the vehement love which
unites contrary wills, and can conform man unto Thee,
the Lover, and in wondrous wise transform him from
brightness unto brightness!'

The soul is now approaching the Unitive Way, but
Hugh alludes to further sufferings. It undergoes a last
stripping of the remnants of self, and it suffers from
longing to see God. It has forsaken the love of sensible
things, but the love of 'intellectual' things must go also.
This is clearly the *Dark Night of the Spirit*. The Transforming
Union is brought about by the Gifts of Understanding
and Wisdom; by the former the soul seizes upon the
highest truth, and by the latter upon the highest goodness.
'Eternity is beginning in the presence of the Beloved. The
interior light is shining; its conversation is in heaven. The
loving soul is still joined to the body, but the south wind
is blowing.' Its faith is such 'that if all the wise of the
world, and all the philosophers declared: "Your faith is not
true faith", the soul would reply: "You are mistaken, and
I alone hold the true faith more happily than by means
of reason and investigations. *I know in whom I have believed.
Who shall separate me from the love of Christ*".'[15]

---

[15] II Tim. 1:12; Rom. 8:35.

V

GERMAN AND FLEMISH MYSTICS

1. TAULER

TO THE SPIRITUAL THEOLOGIANS OF the Rhineland and the Low Countries, Spain was deeply indebted. Some have even maintained that she had no theology of the kind herself until the works of the northerners were known south of the Pyrenees. Though this is an exaggeration, it is impossible to study the works of such as Tauler and Denis the Carthusian, in particular, without discovering how both, especially the former, anticipate St. John of the Cross. When the day came when his teaching had to be defended, these northern mystics were cited, as well as the older authorities, whom we have considered, in proof that he was quite in the sound and orthodox tradition.

Subsequent research has reversed so many earlier opinions upon mediæval books that it is not always easy to be sure as to the effect on Spanish thought of certain individuals. As we have seen, works once assigned to famous writers have turned out to be compilations from several sources, and of such is the popular *Institutions of Tauler*, or the *Medulla animae*. 'More foreigners read Pseudo-Tauler than Tauler,' it has been said. We are told explicitly that St. John used this work, and that he thought highly of Tauler. Several authors have been suggested, but the compiler is now generally held to have been 'Peter of Nijmegen', that is St. Peter Canisius, and the date 1548.

A rather free Latin translation of the eighty-three sermons, which, with a single letter, are the only authentic works of Tauler, was made by the Carthusian, Lawrence Surius, in 1548,[1] and a Spanish translation of the *Institutions*

---

[1] Lawrence Surius was born at Lübeck in 1522, and entered the

is to be found at the end of some treatises by Fr. Seraphin da Fermo, and was published at Coimbra in 1551. By the following year, Surius had translated Ruysbroeck into Latin, and the works of the Franciscan, Henry Herp (Harphius), were known in Spain at the close of the sixteenth century, although, as he died in 1591, St. John may not have read them. From the thirty-fifth chapter of the *Institutions*, John took the now classical 'three signs' whereby it may be known when a soul is nearing the end of the way of 'beginners' and being led to a higher form of prayer than the meditation and affective prayer proper to the Purgative Way.[2]

The work consists of thirty-eight chapters, and lacks both the beauty and vigour of style of the real Tauler, whilst there is much repetition and overlapping, easily explained once we know that it is a collection of excerpts. Chapters 2, 6, 36 and 37 are taken from an anonymous work entitled: *The Imitation of the Life of Poverty of our Lord Jesus Christ*; chapters 9, 10, 11 and 12 are from the *De praecipuis virtutibus* of Ruysbroeck, and chapter 27 from his *De Calculo*. The fourteenth chapter is from Eckhart's[3] *Reden der Unterscheidung*, and the 34th and 38th are extracts from Tauler's *Sermons*. Since the work was studied by St. John and others as Tauler's, it deserves some notice, albeit cursorily, and it may be remarked at once that German

---

Charterhouse of Cologne—noted for its high spirituality and learning—in 1542, after having studied both at Frankfort-on-the-Oder, and the university of Cologne, where he had Peter Canisius as a fellow student, and met John Lanspergius. He died in the same monastery in 1578. He translated Tauler, Ruysbroeck and Suso, but is chiefly known for his *Lives of the Saints*.

[2] 2 *Ascent*, B. II, cc. 13-17; *Dark Night*, B. I, c. 9, and summarily in *Points of Love*, 40 (Peers trans.).

[3] John, 'Master' Eckhart was born c. 1260 at Hocheim, near Gotha; entered the Dominican Order when young, and in 1298 was Prior of Erfurt. In 1300, he went to Paris and took his degree, and though recalled to Germany, soon returned to Paris in 1307, where he was one of the defenders of St. Thomas's doctrine against the Scotists. He was later Lector in Theology at Strasburg and Cologne, but in 1329 his works were condemned. He died in 1327.

mysticism rests upon St. Thomas, Tauler and Suso, though the Flemings are rather Augustinian.

The author begins by reminding his readers of the truth of the divine indwelling and its consequences; he treats briefly of mortal and venial sin and, in language similar to that of St. John, explains how the secret of sanctity is that the human will should become one with the divine will. The soul must never lose sight of the Passion and must aim at utter detachment both from creatures and from sensible devotion, and become 'dead and annihilated to all that is not God'. With the fourth chapter, we come to contemplative prayer, but in the third he has already mentioned 'a divine contemplation which is not disturbed by any image of creatures', and we note that for him, as for others later, 'contemplation' is now synonymous with 'contemplative prayer'. He says that, besides this 'death' which the soul brings about through its own efforts, aided by grace, there is another, reached by unknown ways, arid and dark, through which God normally causes those He loves to pass. We have here the Dark Night of the Senses. In this state, the soul must hold on, waiting continually upon God and seeking no consolation elsewhere. Hitherto it *meditated* upon the Passion; now it honours the Passion by its *state* and lives it.

He proceeds to mention certain obstacles to further progress, which recall St. John's penetrating analysis, and returns to the 'one-ing' of God's will and that of the soul: 'As I have no will but God's, He wills what I will; and in this way I share in His light, which enlightens me and makes me one spirit with Him.'[4] In the seventh chapter, we have some ascetic rules for guarding the senses and are urged to constant prayer, in which we progressively get rid of all 'image-making'. 'In simple, hidden, and super-natural manner, in holy obscurity, they rest; free from all illusion, and tasting a deep peace in this *nothing*—the

---

[4] Compare *Ascent of Mount Carmel*, B. II, c. 5.

Spanish *nada*—in which they are buried. Hidden in the wounds of Christ, they seek only to please God by completely renouncing themselves, and they always choose the lowest place, so that one could not make them fall lower.'

But, let not man deceive himself through self-complacency, and imagine himself a stabilized saint, for a soul can fall even from the heights, and all must beware of resisting the Holy Spirit. Readers are warned that there is no real perfection in revelations, visions and sensible consolations. The last-named are for beginners and the weak, and as souls grow stronger they are deprived of consolations and must learn to live by faith. So many fail to progress owing to futile occupations and frivolous talk, over-familiarity with others, etc. Let a man get rid of anxieties, fears, pleasures and love of earthly things. Let him also leave his private devotions to enter into the eloquent silence and obscurity wherein God will make him realize his nothingness, and that of creatures, in that 'superessential light' which never goes out, and in which God is found.

We now come to John Tauler himself, surely one of the most attractive of mystics. It is impossible to read his sermons without carrying away the impression of a saintly priest and religious, steeped in the spirit of his Order; a genial, gentle person, who could yet be very uncompromising when necessary, and one who had personal experience of God's ways with souls, as learnt in his own case as in those of others. He possesses an insight into human nature not inferior to that of the Mystical Doctor himself; his style is often sheer beauty, whilst his homely illustrations and sense of humour are additional attractions.

A Rhinelander, he obviously liked to walk by the riverside and watch the shipping, and he likens a fervent, steadfast soul to 'a ship well loaded with thoughts of the Beloved and devout works, so that her rudder is deep down in the water'—hence she steers well—'and wafted

along by the wind of love, which is driving her home-
ward unto the Godhead, all prosperously and according
to her longing desires.' Again: 'There are souls who make
as much of small trials as though the Rhine were overflowing through their house.' Elsewhere, the spiritually
slothful are likened to 'good-for-nothing hounds, who
care nothing for the hunt, but lag behind the rest of the
pack and stray away.'

He was born at Strasbourg, probably about 1304, of
well-to-do parents, and entered the Dominican priory
there, sometime between his fifteenth and twentieth
birthdays. He was fervent, loved the observance and was
most anxious to 'do everything'; but he tells us he was
delicate and, at least in his student years, had to accept
dispensations which were a sore trial. (No credit is to
be attached to the story of his 'conversion' by a layman.
All the facts are against it, and obviously no conversion
in the sense there related was ever needed.) He was
sent to the Studium Generale at Cologne, and probably
returned to Strasbourg afterwards. Although it is not
certain whether he met Eckhart at Cologne, he certainly
followed the latter as his Master, although he never fell
into his errors. What is certain is that by 1336, when still
in his thirties, he was already known as an outstanding
preacher and spiritual guide, and had much to do with
the Dominican nuns, who were instructed and directed
by some of the most learned friars in the Province. He
lived later at Cologne and, for some time, at Bâle, where
he was associated with the confraternity known as the
'Friends of God'. He probably refers to this sojourn when
he tells his congregation at Cologne that he was 'once in
a country where the laity are so devout and steadfast that
the word of God produces more fruit there in a year than
it does at Cologne in ten!' However, he commends the
latter city for its devotion to the Blessed Sacrament and
to the practice of frequent Communion, of which latter
he was a strong advocate. He died at Strasbourg in 1361.

He suffered owing to the difficult period in which
he lived: that of 'Babylonish Captivity' of the Avignon
Papacy, when there was a widespread demand for Church
reform and a renewal of the spiritual life, and groups
of earnest folk sometimes overstepped the frontiers of
orthodoxy. He was known as a friend of Eckhart, whom
Luther and other Protestants have hailed as a Reformer
before the Reformation, and others as a Hegelian born out
of due time. True, Tauler, like his contemporaries, merely
used certain words and expressions which were already
common in their day, and dated from earlier times; but
during periods of intellectual and spiritual ferment lesser
men are apt to become panic-stricken, and go in for a
sort of witch hunting, in which blameless and admirable
persons are attacked equally with the blameworthy. It was
the age of decadent Scholasticism, and even professed
Thomists had lost something of the clear thinking and
speaking of their Master. The mystical writers of the time
were fond of such words as 'superessential', and some of
them claimed that by 'superessential contemplation' God
grants to souls sufficiently prepared an intuitive vision of
His Essence. Both Eckhart and Ruysbroeck, as also their
contemporary Harphius (Henry Harp),[5] constantly used
the word, which eventually became to some theologians
among their opponents as the proverbial red rag to a bull,
but to many, including Tauler, it meant merely 'supernatural', or 'supereminent'. It was a literal translation of the

---

[5] The ominous 'superessential' caused the great work of the English
Capuchin mystic, and confessor of the Faith, Benet Fitch of Canfield, the *Reigle de Perfection*, to be forbidden by the Holy Office
in 1594.

Harphius was first Rector of the *Brethren of the Common Life* in
Holland, but became a Franciscan at Rome in 1450. He was later
in office in Cologne and Mechlin, where he died in 1478. He
wrote a widely read Mystical Theology, which was subsequently
corrected and permitted, the word 'supereminent' being substituted
for 'superessential'.

This thorny subject is treated at length in *Surnaturel*, by P. Henri
de Lubac. (Aubier, for the Theological Faculty of Lyons.)

Flemish word *uberweselich*, used by Ruysbroeck, and as he and Eckhart were ontologists as regards their metaphysics, they meant it differently from the Dominican. Everything really depended upon the sense in which this and other offending words were used, as also upon their context. Other such expressions were 'idleness', 'good idleness', 'doing nothing', 'thinking of nothing', 'annihilating oneself', etc., etc., etc. Some of them had been used since Victorine days. The celebrated Denis the Carthusian, against whose orthodoxy never a word was breathed, uses 'superessential' sometimes, and so do other highly respected writers. However, later on, faced with the scandal of Molinos, and other such cases among the Spanish Quietists, orthodox theologians, in Spain, as in the north, took alarm. In 1529, Valdés prohibited Tauler's works in Spain, and subsequently Quiroga, the Carmelite Provincial, renewed the prohibition for the Discalced Carmel.[6] Tauler did not live to see his works suffer thus, and his rehabilitation was prepared by the Spanish mystics, above all by St. John of the Cross.

We turn now to consider his teaching on prayer and the spiritual life. The Sermons were addressed to different classes of hearers, and not all are relevant to our purpose, though Tauler did not hesitate to set a high standard before the laity, and did not think even the graces of contemplative prayer to be the preserve of religious only. He assumes that beginners will use meditation of some kind, especially upon the life and Passion of Our Lord, but he allows wide liberty of spirit.

> Remember that all cannot pray wholly with spiritual acts of the mind, for many must pray with words. Pray as thou canst ... then when thou

---

[6] Joseph of Jesus-Mary (Quiroga) was born at Castre Caldelas, near Astorga, in 1562, being nephew to Cardinal Quiroga of Toledo, and also related to two of the family of St. Teresa. He entered the Carmel of Madrid in 1595, and died at Cuenca in 1629. He became the historian of the Reform, was a strong Thomist and in his own writings cites both Tauler and Ruysbroeck.

findest any manner of prayer very productive
of devotion...keep to that, whether it be the
sorrowful thought of thy sins, or anything else
whatever. Ask of God that prayer which pleases
Him best, and will serve thy soul's best interests.
After having done that, accept whatever devout
thoughts are before thee, whether they be of the
Godhead simply, of the Blessed Trinity, or of the
sufferings of Christ.[7]

Beginners should not reject sensible devotion, for it
has its purpose, neither should they banish the use of
the imagination—'images'—prematurely. Tauler inveighs
against a plethora of devotions and vocal prayers, however,
when such are not of obligation. 'External and showy
exercises of religion prevail greatly nowadays', he remarks—
drily, we feel sure![8] Nor does he approve of elaborate
methods, which were creeping in at his period.

His teaching on detachment and self-abnegation is
precisely that of the Carmelite Doctor. Hand in hand with
prayer, goes progressive purifying of one's intention. God
must be sought, not the consolations of God; God, and
not our thoughts of Him. 'The true and faithful servant
of God goes ever onward, consolation or no consolation,
pleasure or pain, plenty or want; ever straight forward,
through all these things, to God's own self.'[9] The soul
must strive to become a saint for God's sake, and in the
degree of sanctity He decrees for it.'[10]

As the soul progresses, its prayer simplifies, and we
have the prayer of 'loving attention' of St. John of the
Cross; later to be known as acquired contemplation. When
meditation and the affective prayer which develops from
it, have done their work, the soul desires

---

[7] Serm. for Rogation days.
[8] Serm. 17th Sunday after Trinity and 3rd Sunday of Lent.
[9] Serm. for Septuagesima.
[10] Second Serm. 23rd Sunday after Trinity. (Sundays are reckoned
after Trinity, as was the case in pre-Reformation England.)

to betake itself to prayer like a man with water
before him, and drinks sweetly without effort,
without the need of drawing through the channel of previous reflections, forms, and figures.
When thou art aware of this drawing, let no
pious method or practice of thy own devising
hold thee back; but without form or image yield
thyself lovingly to Him, as an instrument in His
hands. If He is allowed His way, then in less time
than it takes to say a Paternoster He will sanctify
thee, and thereby give honour to Himself more
than thou canst do by a hundred years of thy
devotions in the two former ways.[11]

But one day the heavens fall, and this happy state ends
without the soul being able to account for it. Meditation
becomes simply impossible; aspirations fall flat; the soul
is aware only of what has been well called: 'a dull hunger
for God', and, as says St. John of the Cross, 'dwells upon
God with painful care and solicitude, thinking that it is
not serving Him, but is backsliding, because it finds itself
without sweetness of the things of God'.[12]

Tauler comments upon the same *Dark Night of the Senses*
in a sermon on John 10:22: *And it was winter.*[13] Having
spoken of the 'winter' of a soul in grievous sin, he goes
on: 'But there is another winter. This is suffered by a
really God-fearing man. He is mindful of God and loves
Him, and is careful to avoid all sin. But God seems to
have forsaken him, as far as his feelings go; he is dry,
and cold, devoid of all heavenly consolation and spiritual
sweetness.' Again, preaching on John 16:7: *It is expedient for
you that I go*, he says: 'A time comes when God seems lost
and gone... a state of intolerable oppression of spirit; the
soul is desolate, darkened, disconsolate, for God is veiled
from its sight.'[14]

---

[11] First Serm. for Low Sunday.
[12] *Dark Night*, B. I, c. 9, n. 3.
[13] Serm. 2nd Sunday after Easter.
[14] Serm. 4th Sunday after Easter

And Tauler explains the new situation thus:

> Must I actually be in darkness? I answer:
> 'Undoubtedly. Thou art never better off than
> when thou art sunk in the darkness of unknow-
> ing. When thou hast given up thy own willing
> and knowing, then does God enter into thee, and
> then lights up thy soul with His presence ... and
> when He thus comes to thee, he will bring with
> Him everything which thou hast renounced for
> His sake, increased a thousandfold, to be known
> and enjoyed by thee in a new and all-embracing
> form.'[15]

He draws attention, likewise, to the fact that this 'Night' can spread beyond prayer time strictly speaking; so that spiritual reading—even once favourite books—conferences, retreats, etc., etc., seem all equally 'weary, flat, stale and unprofitable'. 'This departure is nothing else than leaving us in utter abandonment, void of comfort, incapable, so that we become dull, heavy, cold and dark with respect to all good works.'[16]

All readers of St. John's *Dark Night* know the chapters wherein he deals with the faults of those whom God is about to purify in the Night of the Senses, classifying them under each of the capital sins. Tauler had pointed them out before him, and in language so similar that obviously there is more than mere coincidence involved. In sermons evidently preached to religious, we hear of the spiritually avaricious, the spiritually gluttonous, the proud, the slothful, etc. We meet the people who 'are forever changing their confessors, seeking advice, ever ready to instruct and admonish their neighbours', although they are the first to resent anything of the kind themselves; those who are continually taking up new devotions, and going in for 'fine spiritual talk'. All are there, just the same in Germany as in Spain!

---

[15] Serm. 1st Sunday after Epiphany.
[16] Serm 4th Sunday after Easter.

Time goes on, the faithful soul progresses, and anon there shuts down the other *Night*—that of the spirit.

> The faculty of love in man thirsts for suffering for the sake of the Beloved, however much one's reason may revolt against it. And hence those favoured souls have a longing to suffer....They thirst for the Cross of Christ, and to them every day is, in very deed, the feast of Holy Cross. And their longing is satisfied. God casts upon the soul the most awful darkness of woe; the most terrible sense of abandonment,[17]

and Tauler tells us that the soul is thus ascending to God by the shortest way, the straight, sheer, path labelled *Nada*—Nothing—in St. John's famous sketch. Like the Carmelite again, he explains how the soul suffers from the very brightness of the light of God; from its inability to love Him as it would; when the strange words of the Dominican Tertiary poet, Michael Field, seem verified:

> And I wonder if love so great
> Will not keep us forever asunder!

Repeatedly, Tauler bids the soul hold on and be faithful to prayer and self-discipline: 'Real devotion is an interior clinging to God Himself, with a soul wholly ready to possess all things, and to think of all things, just as God does.'[18]

And the end is the Transforming union.

> Now God comes, and with His finger touches the well-filled vessel of His graces. The soul is now united to God without any intermediary, and loses itself in Him; will, love, knowledge, all overflow into God, and are lost in Him and made one with Him. The eternal God loves Himself in this soul, all of whose works are done by Him.[19]

---

[17] Serm. for the feast of the Visitation.
[18] Third Serm. for Ascension.
[19] Second Serm. 4th Sunday after Trinity

> Thou must, without doubt, suffer greatly, and
> in all peacefulness die totally to self; there is no
> escape. Ascend, therefore, high up into God's holy
> will; deny thyself in all things, both of spirit and
> of flesh.... O children, how happy shall such a
> man be, when he thus dwells in Jerusalem, the
> city of peace! Full of peace it is indeed, even amid
> this dire unrest; for in this soul's depth is born
> the essential peace of God, coming out of God's
> own abyss of truth and love.[20]

Tauler is as thoroughgoing and all-inclusive as John.
It is the same doctrine of *Nada—Todo*: surrender all to
possess All! 'It is a hard death to the soul when all natural
lights in it, and all its faculties go out in darkness, and
yet a harder death when the bright rays of light shed by
God's own gifts must be quenched in darkness.' Since at
this stage extraordinary graces may possibly be received,
Tauler has strong warnings against asking for such, seeking
revelations, visions, etc., reminding his hearers that imagination plays odd tricks, and how there is not the slightest
merit in such phenomena, but considerable danger. The
transforming union lies not in such, but in absolute conformity to the divine will. He has some sublime passages
respecting this union:

> Surrender thy will to God in all things. Busy
> thyself only with longing for the all-lovely will
> of God! And if thou hast no longing, yet long
> to have a longing.... [21]

> No matter what thou seest or hearest, it all
> comes to thee sanctified by the divine genera-
> tion in thy soul. Everything becomes, as it were,
> God to thee, for thou knowest and lovest nought
> but God.[22]

---

[20] Third Serm. for Ascension.
[21] Serm. for the Circumcision. The 'infinite desire' of Tauler's
sister in St. Dominic: St. Catherine of Siena!
[22] Serm. for 1st Sunday after Epiphany.

Then God leads him ineffably above all captivity to divine freedom in His own self; and
makes him in a certain way rather a divine than
a human being....Herein are all his wounds
healed, all his debts paid, and he has passed
out of creatures into God. His natural state has
in a manner been changed into a divine state.
This blessed exchange is beyond comprehension,
beyond sensible perception and feeling, for it is
beyond natural conditions....We had better be
silent about this than discourse thereof; better
experience it than comprehend it.[23]

Lastly, Tauler and John have another feature in common: both stress the apostolic side of the contemplative life, even if the individual lives a hidden life in a
monastery. It is not merely that such make up for the
lack of active apostolic work by extra prayer and penance,
but the degree of their union with God, the intensity
of their charity, is of immense benefit to the Mystical
Body as a whole. Previously to Tauler, this consideration
is not often found, and never so clearly. Hugh of Balma
suggests it, but it was reserved for Tauler and St. John
to bring it out prominently. The latter states the case in
a celebrated passage.

A very little of this pure love is more precious
in the sight of God, and of greater profit to the
Church, even though the soul appears to be doing
nothing, than all those works taken together. Let
those then, who are great actives, that think to
convert the world with their outward works and
preaching, take note here that they would bring
far more profit to the Church, and be far more
pleasing to God (apart from the good example
they would give) if they spent even half this time
abiding with God in prayer, even had they not
reached such a height as this...since their prayer
would be of such great deserving, and they would

---

[23] Serm. for the Circumcision.

have such spiritual power by it. To act otherwise
is to hammer vigorously, and to accomplish little
more than nothing, at times nothing at all; at
times, indeed it may even do harm.[24]

Tauler speaks thus of 'those chosen spirits whose every
work is divinized':

Upon them, as a house upon its foundation,
stands Holy Church. If they were not in Christendom, Christendom could not stand. The fact
of their very existence among us, that they simply
are, is of more honour and of greater benefit to
Holy Church than a whole world of action by
other Christians.[25]

The work of perfect love is more fruitful to a
man's own soul, and the souls of all other men,
with whom he deals, and it brings more glory to
God than all other works, even if these be free
from mortal sin but are done in a state of weaker
love. The mere quiet repose of a soul with perfect
love is of more worth to God and man than the
active labours of another less perfect soul.[26]

There is God Himself, acting, dwelling, ruling,
granting the soul an incomparable divine life.
Into this life the soul melts away; into the infinite
light and fire of love that God is by essence
and by nature. Back and forth into this relation
with God does such a man pass in prayer, as he
pleads for every necessity of all Christendom; his
holy petitions, his deep yearnings ever guided by
God Himself.... The needs of every soul in Holy
Church are not beyond his help by counsel as well
as by prayer. And yet such favoured souls do not
always pray explicitly for this or that person or
object, but with a certain kind of wide-sweeping,
universal, and yet most simple prayer, do they

---

[24] *Spiritual Cant.* (B), S. 8.
[25] First Serm. for the feast of St. John the Baptist.
[26] Serm. for 1st Sunday after Epiphany.

embrace all souls of men....They see all in the same divine abyss: God's love...viewing thus, as in one glance, the needs of all Christians....To themselves they may seem to be in and out of God in their soul's movements, and yet they are ever in Him, deep in the calm of fathomless love; therein is their life and being; therein all their life's activity....These are noble souls, necessary for Holy Church, sanctifying and consoling all men, giving honour to God.[27]

2. DENIS THE CARTHUSIAN

AMONG THE MYSTICAL WRITERS OF THE later Middle Ages, by far the most prolific is the saintly and gracious Carthusian monk, called the 'Ecstatic Doctor' and 'the last of the Scholastics', the Fleming, Denis van Leeuwen, or Loewis. He was born in 1402 at Rychel, near Saint Trond, in territory then included in the Prince-Bishopric of Liége. He was well educated and owns that his success at school and at the university aroused intellectual ambitions; but he was also very devout and clear-sighted, and whilst in his teens felt drawn to the Carthusian life. He applied to the Prior of Roermund, but since that Order would not accept postulants whom it considered too young to know their own minds, the said Prior advised the boy to continue his studies and return later. Hence Denis went to the University of Cologne, studied philosophy, theology and Scripture, took his degree, and entered Roermond Charterhouse in 1423. From the first, he was outstandingly fervent, and was soon recognized as a great contemplative, his intellectual work never, so we are told, hindering his prayer and his perfect observance.

His output was enormous, filling twenty-five folio volumes in earlier times and more thick quarto ones in the fine modern edition. All the time, he was favoured with contemplation of a very high order, occasional

---

[27] Serm. for Sunday in the Octave of the Ascension.

extraordinary graces which he received with the utmost simplicity, and after forty-eight years of religious life, died in the odour of sanctity in 1471. His last work, the *De Meditatione*, was written in 1469, and the remaining two years of his life were spent in great suffering. Even in an Order which has always made it a rule not to take steps for the beatification of its members, and in which the simple words: *Laudabiliter vixit*—he lived in a praiseworthy manner—are the highest eulogy every bestowed, Denis is informally called 'Venerable', whilst a life of him is to be found in the Bollandists. St. Francis de Sales and St. Alphonsus used to call him 'Blessed', whilst in Spain he was greatly revered. Among those who thought most highly of him was Blessed John of Avila, St. Teresa was influenced by his works, St. John of the Cross used him, and three Spanish editions of his books appeared between 1491 and 1498.

That he should be in high favour with the Carmelites is to be expected, for their relations with the Carthusians were cordial—perhaps too much so from one point of view, for not a few of the most exemplary of the former passed over to the latter. As is well known, the young John of St. Mathis was about to follow his predecessors to the Charterhouse of Paular, when Providence arranged that the tall, imposing Fray Antonio de Héredia, who had similar aspirations, should meet St. Teresa, and consent to become 'the friar and a half' with which the Reform of the Carmelite friars was begun.

Denis is easy to read, although not all his work is of equal quality. His thought and language have the clarity and simplicity of the best Scholastic writing, and we miss the repetition, excessive symbolism and verbosity which often make the Victorines, and even later authorities difficult to follow. He is a great traditionalist, rather than an original writer. Like the Carmelite, Baconthorpe, he draws upon every source within his reach, yet cannot be definitely assigned to any school. Usually, he follows St.

Thomas, for whom he has the deepest respect, and we meet the language of the *Summa* constantly; but he has a high opinion also of 'the devout Doctor', that 'illustrious and divine man' St. Bonaventure.[28] He cites the Victorines frequently, and eulogises his fellow-countryman, Ruysbroeck, and 'that glorious and contemplative man', Denys 'the Areopagite'. He has Holy Scripture at his fingers' ends, is deeply read in the Fathers, and well acquainted with Classical authors. Evidently he knew Greek, and we find him using the ancient work *theoria* for contemplative prayer.[29]

He wrote three treatises: *De Meditatione, De Oratione* and *De Contemplatione,* but his teaching on prayer is far from being confined to these. It is to be found in a number of smaller works, not least a beautiful one: *De Fonte lucis ac semitis vitæ*—the fountain of light and the paths of life—and much to be found in St. John is anticipated. Denis retains the traditional division of prayer, but does not cling to them too closely. Like the first Discalced Carmelites, he is respectful of the nomenclature of past centuries, even though it does not always seem the best.

His treatise on Meditation need not detain us, for it follows the lines we have seen elsewhere. In a small work,[30] he remarks that 'thought' is easy, and does not involve labour; meditation is laborious, since we must do some steady thinking[31] and ponder over the subject, whilst contemplation is attained after having frequently practised meditation until a habit has been formed, but a divine enlightening is needed also. Obviously, he refers to acquired contemplation. He elsewhere expressly alluded to *the acquired grace of contemplation.* 'Moreover, to the contemplative life belong mental and vocal prayer'—he uses the former in the modern sense—'especially when poured

---

[28] *De Cont.*, t. XLI, L. II, art. 9 and 28; *De Fonte Lucis,* t. XLI, art. 16.
[29] *De Fonte Lucis,* t. XLI, art. 17.
[30] *De Perf. Carit.,* t. XLI, art. 4.
[31] In his *De Vita inclusarum,* he supplies some nuns with eight points for meditation on the Passion.

forth in secret; inasmuch as thereby the grace of contemplation is *acquired* and the obstacles thereto removed.'[32]

Like his contemporaries of the *Devotio Moderna* school, but also like Bernard, Bonaventure and Tauler, the Carthusian has a tender devotion to Our Lord, and notwithstanding his admiration for Pseudo-Denys, constantly emphasizes that at no stage of the spiritual life is the Sacred Humanity, above all the Passion, to be excluded. 'Christ is all, during all the Ways. According to His Divinity, He is our end, and according to His Humanity our way.'[33]

Under the heading of Prayer—*oratio*—he includes all prayer of petition 'for those things which it is fitting to ask from God',[34] and also thanksgiving, and, as we read on, it is increasingly obvious that in his opinion, 'prayer' is no stage in the spiritual life, nor is it a mere division, as with some earlier writers, but goes on deepening and developing in purity of intention to the end. It includes petition for the highest union with God, and all that pertains thereto; all affective prayer, and even the Liturgy. No writer has more completely integrated the different forms of prayer than has Denis the Carthusian. And he included also one significant subject which we should not find at an earlier period, and which reflects the grave times in which he lived. Hugh, Richard and Bonaventure remind their readers to pray for the conversion of sinners and heretics; Tauler castigates certain features of religion in his day; Denis urges prayer for the reformation of the Church.

He prescribes no special method, but leaves everyone free to pray as suits him best, remarking that all will pray differently, but he emphasizes the importance of both remote and proximate preparation, and fidelity to private prayer, be it sensibly consoled or no, so that in time the good habit is so formed that it would never occur to the subject to omit it.[35]

---

[32] *De Cont.*, t. XLI, L. 8, art. 12.
[33] *De Med.*, passim, and *De Fonte Lucis*, t. XLI, art. 2.
[34] *De Orat.*, t. XLI, art. 2 and 3.
[35] *De Orat.*, t. XLI, art. 25.

He recognizes the aridity which will set in, sooner or later, and describes it remarkably like St. John of the Cross. He never suggests that it is caused by sin; on the contrary, it is sent to devout and virtuous souls, and he also remarks on the painful anxiety of the soul, so fearful that it has been backsliding that it seems useless to pray and, like all theologians, warns such sufferers that they must on no account yield to this temptation.[36]

He ends the *De Fonte lucis* with a list of the features which should mark the contemplative who is in earnest. Such a one must be faithful to prayer, to self-examination, to the practice of the presence of God; he must carefully avoid occasions of sin and watch over his senses; he must ponder on the Passion, and invoke the angels and his patron saints; he must study his own character and temperament, and train himself accordingly; he must cultivate discretion and fraternal charity, and he must frequently consider the great grace of a religious vocation and, in St. Paul's words: strive to walk worthy of it.[37] He must aim at continual recollection, and if his work is too absorbing for the simultaneous practice of interior prayer, at least let him pause every now and then and turn to God. When he actually betakes himself to prayer, it is preferable that such prayer should be silent, though Denis allows that vocal prayer may be a help from time to time. When devotion fails completely, then short but very frequent prayers should be said.[38]

He is very reasonable, and advises a posture which may make it easier to pray; and though he might be more exacting than the English hermit, Richard Rolle, he does not object to a sitting position if such is really helpful, but he prefers that one should remain still. Singularity is to be avoided, as also any 'showing off' —*ostentatio*—which may attract attention. 'Do not groan, sigh, strike your breast, or

---

[36] *Ibid.*, t. XLI, art. 23.
[37] Eph. 4:1-3.
[38] *De Orat.*, art. 25, and *De Cont.*, L. II, art. 19.

stretch out your arms!'[39] Above all, the soul should cherish
an abiding sorrow for sin, and remember that the *Miser-
ere* is one of the best of prayers for, as Denis reminds us,
Hugh of St. Victor says we fly to God on the wings of our
compunction and His mercy. As so often with Denis, we
find the blending of the old and the new—we might almost
call him a 'transitional' writer—for compunction was ever a
favourite virtue of the traditional monastic spirituality. The
highest form of prayer, however, is praise, and we should
praise God not only for His benefits and loving-kindness,
to us and to all men, but supremely for being *Himself*:[40]
'for being God', as with that uncanny insight sometimes
granted to children, a small girl known to the present
writer once put it. *Gratias agimus tibi propter magnam gloriam
tuam.* One last piece of advice brings us naturally to the
subject of contemplation: it is well to prolong one's private
prayer, if free to do so, but duties binding by obedience
must not be omitted in order to pray 'over-time'—'unless,
perchance, the prayer ends in a rapture!'

When we come to Denis's teaching on contemplation,
again we note the 'originality' of the bringing forth new
things and old. Conservative and humble as he is, he cites
the old definitions of the Victorines but does not really
use them much, and supplies some definitions of his own.
Like others, he is trying to treat of contemplation and
mystical prayer under one heading. The Carmelites do so,
in the end, and the two are now treated as synonyms for
practical purposes, but it is not possible to do so when
dealing with the mediævals. For them, contemplation is an
intellectual process, which may and should end in what we
now call mystical prayer; and as the said writers were holy
men, and all, seemingly, experienced infused contemplation
as we now call it, they assumed that all souls would fare
likewise, if they corresponded with their graces. Their
glowing descriptions really refer to their prayer, but not,

---

[39] *De Orat.*, t. XLI, art. 27
[40] *Ibid.*, art. 31, and *De perf. Carit.*, t. XLI, art. 22.

strictly, to what they call contemplation, which even Denis defines as what amounts to simplified meditation, but on 'the Blessed Trinity, the superessential and simple Godhead, and the Incarnation'.[41] Like the Carmelites, he uses the term *Mystical Theology* as synonymous with contemplative prayer,[42] and in his *Dialogue on the perfection of charity*, states that in mystical theology, contemplation, meditation and thinking can be called one really existent thing, but are much to be distinguished in essence, or definition.[43] He thus draws the Scholastic distinction between things which are really separable, and those which are separable only in thought. Elsewhere, he tells us that the contemplative life means setting oneself untiringly to know the supreme and uncreated Truth, to search into the things of God, and the beatitude of the eternal and adorable Trinity; and also to be enkindled with love of the highest Good, and to rest in God by means of contemplation and love.[44] It is the same twofold conception of contemplation as 'intellectual' and 'sapiential', found in St. Bonaventure—who yet avoided defining contemplation at all—and one feels, as evidently does Denis, that somehow it is not satisfactory. After all, not all brilliant theologians were, or are, mystical contemplatives. One might know the *Summa*, and all the standard theological treatises backwards, and satisfy the most exacting examiners *summa cum laude*, but that need not produce five minutes of infused contemplation! Something more is needed, and there remains the question of the simple and unlearned who, according to the Seraphic as to the Ecstatic Doctor, can reach the loftiest heights of prayer, given the grace. St. Teresa is nearer to solving the problem when she teaches that infused contemplation is

---

[41] *De Cont.*, L. I, t. XLI, art. 16.

[42] *Ibid.*, L. II, art. 11. 'The highest kind of contemplation possible in this life is the unitive intuition of Mystical theology.'

[43] *De perf. Carit.*, t. XLI, art. 14. *In theologica mystica, scias quod contemplatio, meditatio, et cogitatio possunt dici unum esse in re, quamquam multum differt in ratione.*

[44] *De vita inclusarum*, t. XXXVIII, art. 14.

the 'short cut' to the heights and depths of God, and she also calls it *Mystical Theology*; but one cannot count upon it as a matter of course.

Denis maintains that anyone, even the 'idiots'—the old word which has so changed its meaning!—and women, may aspire to contemplation of the highest order; since to them, as to the learned and the men, God will grant the grace 'of such perfect and holy conversation'.[45] (The *Vita inclusarum*—'Life of Enclosed nuns'—already quoted, was written for Carthusian nuns.) However, he adds a warning that there may possibly be danger 'in overcurious investigation into that theology of the Trinity, especially in the case of women, but even sometimes in that of men'. He goes into no detail, so we do not know whether he feared possible mental overstrain or a lapse from orthodoxy. All will be well, provided such investigation be not 'immoderate' but calm, self-controlled—*sobrie*. Simple love and faith are the necessary conditions, but all must know and believe the doctrinal essentials.[46]

He explains, in the usual way, that contemplation which issues in contemplative prayer is an actuation of the gifts of the Holy Ghost, particularly that of Wisdom,[47] and an experimental knowledge of God by means of a unifying embrace of love. It takes place in the highest part of the soul—*supremus apex*—and is called Mystical Theology.[48] 'Love enters in where knowledge stays without';[49] yet light and love are not separated, for the gift of Understanding works also. Besides the seraphic love, there is the cherubic 'gazing', no longer by merely human investigation, but by the *light* of mystical contemplation:[50] the 'ray of the mystical vision' which God grants now in greater, now in lesser measure as He wills. The heart of the lover is

---

45 *De Cont.*, t. XLI, art. 38.
46 *De Fruct. Temp. Deduc.*, t. XL, art. 12
47 *De Fonte Lucis*, t. XLI, art. 5.
48 *Ibid.*, art. 13.
49 *De Fonte Lucis.*, t. XLI, art. 17.
50 The word used is *theorica*.

transformed in God,[51] for charity is a virtue which assimilates and penetrates, conforming the will of the lover to that of the Beloved. Here he cites Plato and Aristotle, and seems to have Cicero also in mind: a friend is an *alter ego*—another self—and our love of God is a love of friendship—*amicitia non eros*. It is the transforming union of perfect conformity, and ecstasy and extraordinary graces may be granted. There may be rapture, during which 'the soul knows nothing of itself'. In a letter written only under obedience, relating a vision which he had himself, when something affecting his house, and the state of a soul, was revealed to him, Denis speaks with utter simplicity and humility.

As for ecstasy, he regards it as simply a degree of unitive love. Indeed, he considers it synonymous with the latter, and though he allows that this may sometimes weaken the body, he does not seem to think that such a result will necessarily follow, since he holds that 'the contemplation which is without ecstatic and unitive love does not, properly speaking, deserve to be called contemplation, unless it extends also to the affective powers of the soul',[52] Plainly, he does not believe in a contemplation which resides only in the intellective powers. Nor is 'mystical love' a 'natural' affective love towards God, but a love freely and supernaturally infused by Him, who is the vigour and life of the soul, its Mover, Ruler and End.[53] But, like other mediæval authorities, he makes it clear that there need not be any startling outward sign, such as a certain type of religious art has associated with ecstasy. The soul in ecstatic prayer *is* 'outside of itself' for the time being, and absorbed in God; but the body

---

[51] Compare *Spirit. Cant.* (B), S. 39, n. 5, where St. John speaks practically identically. It is interesting to find Denis borrowing the definition of the Trinity of Alanus de Insulis: *Theol. Regulæ*, col. 627, P. L., CCX: 'An intelligible sphere, of which the centre is everywhere and the circumference nowhere.'
[52] *De Perf. Carit.*, t. XLI, art. 5.
[53] *De Cont.*, l. III, art. 16.

may be—probably is—quietly kneeling in church or cell, and unless the subject reveals the fact, those present, if any, need never know what has taken place; the more so since, like all mystics, Denis states that prayer at such a degree is not long.

It is interesting that he does not agree with his elusive brother in St. Bruno, Hugh of Balma, in holding that the will—the *apex affectivus*—may be moved by God without any previous thinking. The Fleming maintains that we must *know* God before we can *savour* Him. The knowledge may not be perceived because of the ardour of love, but some knowledge has preceded that love nevertheless.[54]

3. BLESSED JOHN RUYSBROECK

IT HAS BEEN CLAIMED THAT ST. JOHN OF the Cross was particularly influenced by the Flemish mystic, Blessed John of Ruysbroeck, first a canon of the collegiate chapter of Saint Gudule, at Brussels, and later Prior of the reformed Augustinian house of Groenendael, in the forest of Soignes, and a contemporary of Tauler. But although their works show features in common, there is really little evidence that John was more indebted to Ruysbroeck than to certain others. It has, indeed, been questioned if he had read the Fleming, save in books which are now recognized as compilations by other hands. However, Ruysbroeck was one of those cited in the Carmelite's defence by Fray Basilio Ponce de Leon.

He is generally better known than others whom we have studied, partly because he is another who, quite untruly, has been pronounced a morning star of the Reformation, and his works have been more widely translated into modern languages, and so become more generally familiar. The fact that he has been beatified in relatively modern times has also helped to popularize him, albeit

---

[54] *De Cont.*, t. XLI, l. III, art. 15. In art. 19 Denis reminds us that one who would rise thus high must set himself to please God, 'not in any sort of way' but with a firm purpose. See also l. III, art. 15.

he is not always easy to understand. His works fell under suspicion, as did those of several of his contemporaries, and for similar reasons; yet like St. John, he explicitly protests his perfect loyalty and adherence to the Church's judgement, and Denis the Carthusian praises him for his so doing. 'Finally, as regards all I understand and hold, and all I have written, I submit to the judgement of the saints and of Holy Church. For I will to live and die Christ's servant, in the Christian faith, and with the grace of God I desire to be a living member of Holy Church.'[55]

We find in his works certain features common to the later mediæval mystics, especially to those of the northern lands: a deep devotion to the Sacred Humanity and the Blessed Sacrament, strong approval of frequent Communion, and also a certain practical tone throughout his teaching. He spares us the familiar disquisitions on contemplation as an intellectual exercise, and equates it with mystical prayer, as will St. John. Like the latter, he sometimes expresses his teaching in verse and proceeds to elaborate it in prose; and though as a poet he cannot be compared to the Spaniard, since he is the only mystical writer of the period to do this, it is a strong argument in favour of John's having studied him.

They differ at the outset, however, for Ruysbroeck is not a Thomist. He allows to man's higher faculties a wider field than does St. Thomas, who distinguishes better the natural from the supernatural order. The Fleming holds that if our faculties are strengthened by grace, they have an obediential power of applying themselves to God; but Thomas denies this and teaches that they have only an aptitude to be raised by the divine light. Here Ruysbroeck is following St. Bonaventure and, through him, St Augustine.[56] He sees the spiritual life as a return to God, but nature is always considered as being at the base of the

---

[55] *The Book of most high Truth*, c. 14.
[56] Ruysbroeck, *The Kingdom of the Lovers of God; Summa Theol.* Ia, IIæ, q. 113, art. 10; Bonaventure, Sermo IV. (Quaracchi edn.)

supernatural gifts, which are grafted thereon in virtue of this obediential power.

His metaphysics are those of the ontologists, and he uses two sets of words, if we may so express it, and distinguishes between what is 'supernatural' and what is 'superessential'. For him the former is to the latter as means to an end, or way to term, and the domain of the supernatural is to him an intermediary domain. Man is led supernaturally to his 'super-essence' by the imitation of Christ. The divine image which shines in each created spirit, as in a mirror, must be united to its divine Model; and that will be brought about by striving to resemble that model more and more. God is the 'superessence' of every created being, and life in God is 'superessential' life. Our beatitude, then, is also 'superessential', and the highest degree of contemplation, which he describes as 'union without difference', is a 'superessential state'.[57] To this we must return presently.

His treatment of the *scintilla synderesis* reminds us again of Bonaventure. Other Franciscan features in his works are his Exemplarism, and his strong emphasis on the part of the will, rather than of the understanding, in the soul's spiritual progress. One of his books, the *Seven Steps of the Ladder* of *Spiritual Love*, written for Margaret van Moerbeke, a Poor Clare of Brussels, was suggested by Bonaventure's *Itinerarium*, and contains also a quotation from the *Vitis Mystica*.[58]

His stages of the spiritual life are much like those of St. John of the Cross, except for his very personal language. Beginners are exhorted to cultivate silence and recollection, and to live a retired life—Ruysbroeck lived as a hermit at Groenendael before becoming a religious—persevering in prayer. As time goes on, the characteristic aridity appears, and is called 'darkness', but the author regards it as spiritual discipline, the remedy for which is to abandon

---

[57] See *Surnaturel*, by P. Henri de Lubac, c. IV. (Aubier, Lyons.).
[58] Seven Steps, c. 9; Vitis Mystica, c. 2.

oneself wholly to God. 'God hides Himself with all His graces, and man feels he will never recover health. All consolation coming from creatures is wearisome, and from God's side he no longer feels any savour or joy.'[59] Here we have, almost verbally, St. John's description of the third sign whereby it is shown that the soul has entered into the *Night of Sense*, and Ruysbroeck also asks: 'Why do not all spiritual men reach this?'—only to reply again almost in John's words: 'They do not correspond to the divine motion by self-abnegation. They remain exterior and dispersed; they multiply active works and do not let God have His way.'[60]

We meet the age-old comparisons of the iron in the fire and the sunlight in the air, but here as elsewhere, Ruysbroeck, who had always in mind the Beghards, and other false mystics in Flanders, with their pantheistic teachings,[61] emphasizes that each keeps its own nature, and that man can never become God. In this connection, we come to a point which puzzled even his friends.

In his *Kingdom of the Lovers of God*,[62] he mentions three ways in which the contemplative may be united to God: (1) by intermediary; (2) without intermediary; (3) without difference. The first is simply the union by grace and good works; the second is that of the 'iron and the fire', when the soul's will becomes one with God's will: 'so that all possibility or capability of willing otherwise than as God wills disappears: His will having become ours.'[63] The union *without difference* called forth questions from the brethren of a neighbouring Charterhouse, and to explain it he wrote the *Book of most high Truth*. We see there that he

---

[59] *Book of most high Truth*, c. 6; *Mirror of eternal salvation*, c. 2.

[60] *Ibid.*, c. 6; *Living Flame*, c. 2, n. 27.

[61] The *Brethren of the Free Spirit*, founded in the fourteenth century in Brabant, were the heirs of the Beghards and, like them, held Pantheist doctrine and later became Quietists. They had much in common with the Spanish *Illuminati*.

[62] Chapters 5–9.

[63] *Mirror*, c. 5.

is simply treating of the Spiritual Marriage: the supreme
degree of union and ecstatic love possible in this life: the
transformation in God described by St. John, and the
unusual language is due, as we have already seen, to the
author's metaphysical standpoint, as also to the real difficulty of rendering the exact meaning of his Flemish into
theological Latin.[64] Nevertheless, one can understand the
remonstrances of some Ruysbroeck's friends that, although
his doctrine was orthodox, his style was unsatisfactory.

> Our Lord and the beloved are consummated in
> one, as He is one with the Father in union of
> the Holy Spirit, as Himself prayed might be. The
> soul must not be idle, although it must not be
> given wholly to external works. Reason and the
> senses must yield to faith and the gaze of con-
> templation, but they remain as habits and cannot
> perish, any more than can human nature. The
> spirit clings to God without intermediary until
> it becomes so one with God that it is plunged
> into the superessential unity; and then there is
> union without difference.

Neither nature nor its powers are destroyed, but nature
is subordinated to grace. The result is joy, which will be
complete only in the Beatific Vision.[65] Elsewhere, he tells
us that the Trinity dwells in the soul, continually carrying
on its operations.[66] Again: 'By union we become one
same spirit, one same love, one same life with Him, but
we remain always creatures. For although transformed in
His light and ravished by His love, we recognize and feel
that we are other than he.'[67]

---

[64] As the ontological theory of the structure of the soul, and its
life in God, was abandoned, so was the phraseology, and we do
not find it in the Spanish school. As says P. Bruno de Jésus-Marie,
the author of the well-known biography of St. John of the Cross:
'pour un Jean de la Croix... *la nature ne doit pas seulement être purifée
par la grâce, elle doit être radicalement surélevée.*'
[65] *Kingdom of the Lovers of God*, cc. 5–9.
[66] *Mirror*, c. 19.
[67] *Ibid.*, c. 19

Yet Ruysbroeck's feet are always on the ground, and he is emphatic throughout on the importance of faith. 'Christ has obliged us to live on earth, amidst all His gifts, with a firm faith, and not in bright and glorious contemplation; for it is by integral faith that we merit eternal contemplation.'[68] In another place, he makes a statement which both John and Teresa have echoed: 'God wills to be entirely yours, provided that you will consent to be wholly His, to live and abide in Him as becomes a holy and divine man.'[69]

They have also a minor point in common in that both— and they are alone in so doing until a later period—state that until the soul raised to contemplation settles down into 'quiet peace' its behaviour may seem eccentric to others; and Ruysbroeck remarks that the soul in the state of Transforming union is ever calm, and in the presence of God in 'luminous darkness'.[70]

The Night of the Spirit is dealt with chiefly in the *Adornment of the Spiritual Marriage*, but there is nothing novel in his treatment. He dwells on the soul's suffering from its seeming inability to love God as it should and would, and its longing for Him, and he uses a vivid expression which surely could only have occurred to one who spoke from experience: *The terrible and immense love of God!*[71]

4. THE 'DE ADHAERENDO DEO'

WE MAY END THIS PORTION OF OUR study by noticing another anthology: the *De Adhaerendo Deo*, which in 1414 was assigned by the Spaniard, Luis of Valladolid, to St. Albert the Great, whose life he wrote. Until the beginning of the present century this authorship was almost unquestioned, but important discoveries have

---

[68] *Ibid.*, c. 9.
[69] *Ibid.*, c. 1; *Living Flame* (B) S. III, n. 28; *Way of Perf.*, c. 28, n. 12.
[70] *Book of most high Truth*, c. 8. *Ascent of Mount Carmel*, B. III, c. 2, nn. 4–8.
[71] *Mirror*, c. 17.

established that the work is a compilation from mediæval sources made by Johann von Kastl, Abbot of the Bavarian monastery in that town.[72] Its precise date is unknown, but probably lies between 1384 and 1414. Of its compiler, likewise, little is known, save that he was a religious of outstanding learning and spirituality. We learn from contemporaries[73] that he was a great student of Scripture and 'not unlearned in profane studies', a theologian, philosopher, poet and withal an eloquent preacher. About 1404, he succeeded in reforming his own abbey, which became the centre of a reformed Benedictine Congregation, and the first of a trio of such, of which Bursfeld and Melk were the other members. Another, and original, work of his, the *De lumine increando*, belongs to 1410. Strongly influenced by the great reforming movement of Windsheim, he shows characteristics of the *Devotio moderna* in the *De Adhaerendo*, of which MSS. were found at the abbeys of Melk and Tegensee.

The book, called in English *Union with God*, contains sixteen chapters, of which the third is from the treatise *De Veritate* of the Franciscan, David of Augsburg, whom we know already, whilst the seventh is made up of excerpts from St. Bonaventure's *Itinerarium*, the *Stimulus Amoris*, Hugh of St. Victor and the work *De spiritu et anima*.[74] Kastl also borrows from another Franciscan, Rudolf of Biberach (c. 1360) and from Ruybroeck's *Sparking Stone* (the *De calculo*).

---

[72] The German scholar, Dr. Grabmann, found three MSS. of the complete work attributed to Johann von Kastl. (See *Der Benediktiner mystikes Johannes von Kastl. Tübinger* Theol. Quartelschrift, 1920.)
[73] Such as Abbot John Trithemius, one of those appointed by the Pope to reform the Benedictines in Germany and Italy.
[74] Until the twelfth century, this work was fathered upon St. Augustine, and is printed after his works in Migne, P. L., t. XL, col. 779, but St. Thomas pronounced it to be by some Cistercian, and the Maurists agreed with him, assigning it to Alcher of Clairvaux. The portions taken from the *Stimulus Amoris* are in chapters seven and fifteen of *De Adhaerendo*, and the twelfth chapter contains the borrowings from the *De septem itineribus æternitatis of Rudolf*. The work is thus largely Franciscan.

The first two chapters emphasize the essential need of self-abnegation and recollection.

> A man seeking perfection will attain his object only when, hidden from and forgotten by the world, wholly recollected within himself, he abides in silence in the presence of Jesus Christ.... Strive unwearyingly, with all thy powers, to reach God through Himself: that is through God-made-Man, that thou mayest attain to the knowledge of His Godhead through the wounds of His sacred Humanity.

In chapter three, David of Augsburg tells the reader:

> The soul cannot give itself perfectly at the same time to two objects as contrary one to the other as light and darkness; for he who lives united to God dwells in the light, he who clings to this world lives in darkness.[75]
>
> The highest perfection of man in this life lies in this: that he is so united to God that his soul, with all its powers, and faculties, becomes recollected in Him and is one spirit with Him. Then it remembers nought save God, nor does it relish or understand anything but Him. Then all its affections, united in the delights of love, repose sweetly in the enjoyment of their Creator.

It sounds like an echo, through the centuries, of Richard of St. Victor's *De gradibus violentiæ charitatis*! So does the following chapter, wherein we have the usual advice to cease from the use of imagery:

> At length, he, in a manner, forgets all images, and by a simple and direct act of pure intellect and will, contemplates God, who is absolutely simple.

---

[75] Compare St. John *Ascent*, B. I, cc. 4 and 6. 'Two contraries cannot exist in one person; and that darkness which is affection for creatures, and light, which is God, are contrary to each other.... Affection for God and affection for creatures are contraries, and thus there cannot be contained within one will affection for creatures and affection for God.'

Cast from thee, therefore, all phantoms, images,
and forms, and whatsoever is not God, that all
thy intercourse with Him may proceed from an
understanding, affection, and will alike purified.

Once the soul has entered generously upon this pre-
liminary work, the Holy Spirit will act upon it, and it will
no longer need to study and read the Holy Scriptures to
learn the love of God and its neighbour, for the Spirit
Himself will teach it.

But anon, in the fifth chapter, we are reminded that
we have reached the *devotio moderna,* when there was a
definite tendency to reject intellectual work and concen-
trate on the will:

I had rather feel contrition, than know the definition thereof.
What doth it avail thee to dispute learnedly of
the Trinity, if thou art wanting in humility, and
art thereby displeasing to the Trinity?
If thou knewest the whole Bible, and all the
saying of all the philosophers, what would it all
profit thee, without the love of God and grace?[76]

We have noticed the same tone earlier on, in Hugh
of Balma. The aim of the spiritual writers of this school
was a renewal of the interior life; they rightly wished to
get rid of the formalism which had gone far to sap the
spiritual strength of many a religious house; hence the
reaction against learning, especially since Ockham and
his disciples had done so much damage to Scholasticism;
and the attitude would last for many a day, and have
some less fortunate results in cases of less holy souls. St.
John of the Cross was happily in a country, and attend-
ing a university, which was to be in the forefront of a
Thomist revival.

The sixth chapter contains a description of the Unitive
Way, in the great tradition:

---

[76] *Imitation of Christ,* B. I, c. 1.

The true friend of Jesus Christ ... seeks nothing outside of God, but knows that of a truth, he has found in Him all the good and all happiness of perfection. Then will he be in some measure transformed in God. He will no longer be able to think, love, understand, remember aught but God and the things of God; he will no longer be able to behold himself or creatures, save in God. No love will possess him but the love of God, nor will he remember creatures, or even his own being, save in God.

The seventh chapter, being the most composite, contains a good deal of information. The soul will encounter obstacles, such as distractions, dryness, weariness of spirit and 'darkness'; but it seems the 'bright Darkness', to use Fray Jerome Gracian's description of it, as he experiences it in himself. The description is Dionysian:

Then thy soul will enter into the darkness of the spirit, and will advance further, and penetrate more deeply, into itself. By this means, thou wilt attain more speedily unto the beholding in a dark manner of the Trinity in Unity and Unity in Trinity in Christ Jesus, in proportion as thy effort is more inward.

In the ninth chapter, which is Scholastic in tone, it is rather surprising to find a definite resemblance to the spirituality of the Spaniards, the Benedictine Cisneros and St. Ignatius Loyola. We find the same consideration proposed to us as in the Exercises: our utter dependence upon God, who is preserving us in being; in a sense, is ever creating us from moment to moment; we are because He wills us; left to ourselves we are utterly helpless. We have God put before us as First Cause, eternal Principle. With the twelfth chapter the author returns to the Transforming union. 'Love has the power of unifying and transforming; it transforms the lover into the Beloved, and vice versa; each passes into the other, as far as is possible. The soul is more truly where it loves than where it gives life.'

There is nothing new in the last four chapters, which are nearly all borrowed matter, but the thirteenth treats again of union with the Blessed Trinity as the final goal of prayer, as we find supremely in St. John of the Cross. 'When that union which exists between the Father and the Son, and the Son and the Father shall be found in a man's mind and soul, there is true prayer.'[77]

---

[77] See c, 13: *On true Prayer.*

SPAIN AGAIN, AND
SAINT JOHN OF THE CROSS

I. LATER SPANISH SPIRITUALITY

THERE IS NEITHER NEED NOR SPACE
to dwell at length upon the details of the life of
St. John of the Cross, nor upon his Spanish predecessors and contemporaries. Both tasks have been well
done already,[1] and his debt to them was less than to the
older authorities. We cannot, however, omit them entirely.

The period of the Avignon Papacy had been disas-
trous for Spain as for other countries, although there had
been those who reacted vigorously against the decadence.
There existed a body of 'knightly literature'—the sort of
romances enjoyed by St. Teresa's mother, and for a time
by herself, though she would repent it deeply—but the
Franciscan missionary and orientalist, Raymund Lull, is
the only outstanding name among religious authors, if
we except certain reformers. There was a Latin work, De
Planctu Ecclesiæ—'The lament of the Church'—by another
Franciscan, Fray Alvaro Pelagia, later Bishop of Silves, who
deplores how 'they sell the Body of Christ for money',[2]
and speaks of the decadence of the religious Orders and
clergy in general: their ignorance and low moral standards,
though he makes no mention of heresy.

Others wrote in the same vein, and the outcome was the
setting up of the Inquisition by Ferdinand and Isabella, and

---

[1] See biographies by Lewis, Fr. Bruno, O. C. D., and *Spirit of Flame*
by E. A. Peers. Also *Spanish Mysticism, Studies of the Spanish Mystics*
(2 vols.). *Ramon Lull* and the translation of the *Ascent of Mount Sion*,
by Bernardino of Laredo, O. F. M.
[2] Corpus Christi pro pecunia vendunt. (Doubtless an allusion to
simony.)

the Catholic reform under the Franciscan, Cisneros, later Archbishop of Toledo and Primate of Spain.[3] He began by a visitation of his own Order and his report was severe. A few houses of friars are observant, but are persecuted by the relaxed, whilst the nuns are lukewarm, have too much property, and few observe enclosure. As elsewhere in Europe, the abuses are put down as originally due to the Black Death, and the resulting indiscriminate ordination and profession of subjects without vocation, or at best, with inadequate training and study. Cisneros put down the said abuses drastically, and the reform was generally successful as regards the Regular clergy, but the Seculars were not thoroughly reformed until the Council of Trent. Among the Cistercians, the abbey of Piedra was reformed by its abbot, Martin de Vargas, and the monastery of the same Order, *Monte Sión*, in Toledo, became a centre of strict observance. Other Orders gradually followed their example.

As Spain had a catholic reform, so had she a Catholic renascence. Gradually, there was a revolt against the 'decadent' theology of the late Middle Ages, much of which had become purely fromal, as also against the artificiality of much Scripture study. Such men as Vitoria, Cano, de Soto, Ambrosio Morales, Tomás Morado, Carvajal, and other well-known reformers were strongly in favour of a change, but they were careful not to condemn the great Scholastics along with their later inferior followers, whilst at the same time, they accepted all that was good in Humanism. But they recognized that, to re-convert the northern lands, 'modern methods' would be needed, and they were in favour of scientific study of Scripture, History and Philology.

---

[3] Francisco Ximenes de Cisneros was born at Torrelaguna, New Castile, in 1436, and educated at Alcalá and Salamanca, becoming a Consistorial Advocate at Rome. In 1484 he entered religion at Toledo, and in 1495 was made Archbishop. In 1507, he was created a Cardinal, and died near Valladolid in 1517. He was responsible for the Complutensian Bible of Alcalá, and built the Mozarabic chapel in Toledo cathedral.

The middle fifteenth century sees the emergence of native Spanish writers, mostly ascetic, though some were mystical. Franciscans and Augustinians were to the fore, and it is to be noticed that they tend to write from experience. The one outstanding Dominican, Luis of Granada, has been described as 'a Dominican *malgré lui*', and certainly his fondness for Augustine, his passion for nature, and style, seem more akin to the Friars Minor.

His master and precursor was the great secular priest, Blessed John of Avila,[4] and St. Teresa was influenced by his *Libro de la oración* which she recommended to her nuns. The same may be said of the *Tratado de la Oración*, by St. Peter of Alcantara who, with a scrupulous literary honesty rare in that age, acknowledges that he has taken his material largely from the Dominican. One promising Franciscan, Francisco Ortiz, was unfortunately misled by a *Beata*,[5] Francisca Hernández, who had become an Alumbrada, and in consequence he lost credit and suffered imprisonment on her account. The Augustinian, Luis de Leon, is in a class apart. Very brilliant, he fell under suspicion for a while, but his works were later triumphantly vindicated. He draws much upon Aristotle—one would rather have expected Plato!—and uses Bonaventure, Ruysbroeck and Tauler.

One of the first and most important Spanish Spiritual theologians was García Ximenes de Cisneros, the great Benedictine reformer, and cousin of the Cardinal. Born

---

[4] Born at Almodóvar in 1500, he studied law at Salamanca and theology at Alcalá. Known as the 'Apostle of Andalusia', he died in 1569 and was beatified in 1894. He is a strictly   ascetic writer.
[5] A *Beata* was a devout woman who, without joining a religious Order, lived a retired life, given to religious exercises, under approved direction in her home. Sometimes a group of such would form an informal community, and from one of these the convent of the Incarnation at Avila originated. John of Avila wrote his best-known work, *Audi filia*, for a young court lady, Doña Sancha Carilla, who adopted this kind of life, and St. Mariana of Quito was another such. In South America, the life lingered on until comparatively modern times.

at Cisneros, in Leon, in 1455, and educated at Salamanca, he entered the reformed abbey of Valladolid, *San Benito el Real*, in 1475, a house in which several Englishmen, exiled from their country during Penal times, subsequently followed the vocation they could no longer find in their native land. Twenty years later, he was sent to reform the famous monastery of Montserrat, which, largely owing to an unworthy abbot, had fallen on very evil days and seemed likely to die out. Cisneros succeeded in his task, and became Abbot. In 1499, appeared his *Exercises for the Spiritual Life*, the first ascetico-mystical work of the kind in Spanish, which St. Ignatius doubtless read when at Montserrat. Incidentally, Cisneros was largely responsible for the great popularity of St. Bonaventure's works in Spain at this time: a popularity which may well have had its influence upon St. John of the Cross, when he prescribed them for study in his own Order. The Benedictine's reading was evidently very wide, and he uses not only the Fathers, but the Victorines, Hugh of Balma, and the German and Flemish mystics. He makes it clear that he is writing for such as cannot read Latin but are earnestly seeking union with God. The book was written in both Spanish and Latin and, in its rather complicated method, owes something to the *Rosetum exercitiorum*, a very elaborate and somewhat artificial 'method' drawn up by Jan Mombaer, a Fleming and an adherent of the *Devotio Moderna*.

An outstanding writer was the Franciscan laybrother, and Doctor of Medicine of Paris, Bernardino of Laredo. He was born at Seville in 1482, where he subsequently entered the Friar of *San Francisco del Monte* in 1529, dying there in 1540.

He wrote the *Ascent of Mount Sion*, which probably suggested to St. John the title of the latter's first work. How far he actually influenced the Carmelite is problematical, for though they have features in common this could be explained by their familiarity with the same standard mystical works; but he certainly had a marked influence upon St. Teresa. To him she probably owed her devotion to St. Joseph, for he was responsible for spreading it, and obtained the Decree raising the rank of the feast in Spain. He makes much use of Richard of St. Victor, but more remarkable is his frequent citing of Hugh of Balma, although, like others of his Order, he confuses him with the Franciscan, Henry of Baume, confessor to St. Colette. He always speaks of 'Quiet Contemplation', and compares the life of a soul which has reached the Transforming Union to 'a river flowing onward till it is engulfed in the ocean where it had its beginning: that is, in God.'[6]

Needless to say, we have the old example of the iron in the fire, and

> the same comes to pass with the soul that is made one spirit in God, by God and with God. Whilst not ceasing to be a soul, it is so completely infused in God, so entirely transformed in Him, so like God in the one will which is between them, that there is one willing in them and between them; in which willing, the two things are one only, and in one will only—a will enamoured, converted, submerged, engulfed, and transformed in the most finely refined love, wherein the soul is absorbed and made one with the love which transformed it into itself.[7]

The Augustinian Blessed Alonso de Orozco (1500–1591) is interesting as leaning more to the older tradition. He wrote several books on prayer, two of which, the *Garden of Prayer*, and the *Mount of Contemplation*, he dedicated to Queen Juana of Portugal, sister of Philip II. He advises *lectio divina*, and meditation 'to which contemplation is closely allied'. He also cites St. Thomas's definition of the latter: 'the clear and free knowledge of supreme truth, which is God'. In one work, the *History of the Queen of Saba*,

---

[6] *Ascent of Mount Sion*, B. II, c. 10.
[7] *Epístola*, XI.

which he dedicated to Isabel de la Paz (Valois), third wife
of Philip II, he writes of contemplation:

> Let none think that he merits it, but rather that
> if God gives it, He does so of His great liberality
> and goodness. Whence it comes that the per-
> fect lover of God scarcely remembers when he
> prays that sweetness wherein beginners so greatly
> delight; but to such a point submits his will to
> the will of God, that he gives thanks to the Lord
> as gratefully for dryness as for sweetness.[8]

In this case, we are evidently dealing with mystical contemplation. Another friar, whose treatise: *Arte para servir
a Dios*—the 'Art of serving God'—helped St. Teresa and
was recommended by her, was Alonso of Madrid, and
lastly we come to perhaps the greatest Spanish ascetico-
mystical writer previous to St. John, Francisco de Osuna.
His works consist of five *Alphabets*, each chapter beginning
with a letter of the alphabet, of which the *Third Spiritual
Alphabet* is the one which so greatly helped St. Teresa in
the early days of her spiritual life.[9] We do not know the
date of his birth, but the book appeared in 1527, and he
died about 1540. He had lived at Paris and Toulouse, was
widely read, and had obviously much experience with souls,
besides being a contemplative himself. He has clearly been
a novice master, and there is little in community life, its
human, as well as its divine side, which he does not know.
We catch glimpses of a winning personality. Like John, he
was devoted to his mother, and homely comparisons drawn
from family life show that he must have had a happy
childhood, evidently free from the material sufferings
of the poverty-stricken cottage of little Juan de Yepes. It
may be remarked that Blessed John of Avila forbade the

---

[8] *Obras.*, t. II, p. 503.
[9] The first, written in 1528, is a meditation on the Passion; the
second, belonging to 1530, is purely ascetical; the *third* we shall
study, whilst the fourth is a compendium and abridgement of the
previous three, and the fifth is a book for preachers.

Third Spiritual Alphabet to persons insufficiently instructed in spiritual matters, he being an ascetic and missionary, first and foremost.

As a writer, Osuna is 'untidy', given to digressions and to returning to a subject after having, seemingly, finished with it.[10] Nevertheless, we have here 'the real thing'. His object is 'to help souls to attain union with God', and like John he inveighs against incompetent spiritual guides, and the mistaken advice they often give. He says he is often sorry for beginners, especially such as are afflicted with a novice-master 'who satisfies his conscience by reading a portion daily of some well-known book, and attends to externals'.[11] He speaks also of the religious 'who warp the Rule to suit their own behaviour'.

He has a thorough knowledge of Scripture and, like John of Avila, expects his readers to study the Bible, whilst he has the love of nature of St. John and of his own Father, St. Francis, together with the Franciscan spirit of joy and thanksgiving, and the insistence upon never forsaking the Sacred Humanity, *save under certain conditions, and only for a while*, when a soul is entering upon the way of infused contemplation. Only there did St. Teresa— and St. John—differ from him, and for that reason the former omitted him from her list of approved books for her nuns, greatly as she had benefited from him in other respects. She had the same suspicion of Bernardino de Laredo, though a careful study of both authors leaves the impression that she had not quite understood their meaning, or had, unknowingly, exaggerated it.

He is very practical, and follows the 'classical' lines of ascetic teaching. His two main themes in the Purgative Way

---

[10] Bernardino of Laredo has the same fault, and the result is an occasional contradiction of one statement by a later one. The contemporary English Capuchin mystic and confessor of the faith, Benet Fitch of Canfield, is a glaring example, and this fault probably led to the mistaken impression as to his doctrine, which caused his *Reigle de Perfection* to be condemned by the Holy Office.

[11] C. 8.

are recollection, which must be habitual, and an 'emptying of all created things' which scarcely, if at all, yields to John of the Cross. Some of his warnings might be written by the latter, as the following, against giving way to natural curiosity in the case of a grace: 'Remember this: when you are aware that a grace is being granted your soul, do not at the time give way to curiosity about what it is, or examine it; but open your heart to the divine gift, cleansing it, as far as possible, from the dust of wandering thought, and welcome the interior grace with all the love of your heart.' One remembers how St. Teresa made this mistake during her first vision of Our Lord, in the convent of the Incarnation, and of how St. John reiterates that the one concerned must seize upon the 'fruit'—that is the interior grace—and let the 'rind' or 'husk' drop.[12]

Deeply influenced by St. Bonaventure, Osuna distinguishes clearly between 'speculative', or intellectual contemplation, and 'mystical theology', which is a matter of the will. Another wise warning is:

> Evidently, they are mistaken who continually read or recite vocal prayers, or seek for devout phrases uttered by others, if they think by such means to attain that holy practice which consists wholly in affections and interior movements of the heart. Doubtless such exercises are useful, but they do not suffice. For though they may excite some devotion at the time, yet if the book or vocal prayer be relinquished, it is soon forgotten and the devotion departs and will return only with the use of the book or prayers which prompted it.[13]

Like Tauler, he objects to multiplying vocal prayers not of obligation. On the prayer of Union, he writes: 'When man attains to God in this manner, he becomes one spirit with Him by an interchange of wills; so that neither does man

---

[12] *Ascent of Mount Carmel*, B. II, cc. 11–17; B. III, c. 13; *Life of St. Teresa*, c. 7.
[13] *Alphabet*, Treatise 6.

will anything but what God wills, nor does God draw apart from man's will. But they are at one in all ways, like things that are perfectly united.'[14] St. Teresa teaches likewise.

He once quotes, word for word, a well-known passage from the *Prologue* to the Rule of St. Benedict: 'In process of holy living and faith, the path of God's commandments is run with unspeakable sweetness of love', and comments thus: 'Those who begin to follow Christ by austerities, find the way narrow and difficult at first, and their burden heavy; but by perseverance all is overcome, and the strength it engenders makes the work much easier.' He is full of sound common sense, like Teresa and John, and very encouraging. 'Take Seneca's advice', he says once, 'and do not make yourself miserable before the hour comes, or go to meet misfortunes.'[15]

He follows the usual classification and description, but he does not really understand the Night of the Senses. To him, all aridity is punitive, and though he has heard of the Night of the Spirit, he admits: 'I have never read anything about this kind of sadness, which I believe is the highest of all. I mention it here for the consolation of those who attain to it, or rather those who receive it; for God causes it in the soul, without our fully understanding its origin.'[16] Osuna found it in 'proficients' and the 'perfect', and perhaps in himself; but we still wait for a greater than he to fill in the blanks!

Once he uses words that recall John's reply, shortly before his death, to those who deplored the treatment meted out to him. 'Refer all things to love and draw love from them',[17] says the Franciscan; 'Where there is no love, put love, and you shall draw out love again', says the Carmelite.[18]

---

[14] *Alphabet*, T. 6; *Inter. Castle*, Man. 5; *Life*, c. 31.
[15] *Alphabet*, T. 21.
[16] *Ibid.*, T. 7.
[17] *Ibid.*, T. 16.
[18] Letter from St. John to M. Mary of the Incarnation, in Segovia, July 6, 1591.

2. THE MYSTICAL DOCTOR

> He is a man heavenly and divine ... He is truly
> the father of my soul.... He is very advanced in
> the ways of the spirit; to very great experience
> he adds very profound learning.[19]

> I have found no one like him in all Castile, nor
> is there anyone who inspires souls with such
> fervour on their road to heaven. You should all
> recognize that you possess a priceless treasure in
> that saint. Our Lord has given him special grace
> for such guidance.[20]

> He has Our Lord's own spirit.[21]

Such was St. Teresa's opinion of the young friar, 'small in
stature, indeed, but great in the sight of God', who became
the spiritual father of the Reformed Carmel.

When we come to St. John of the Cross, 'the greatest
metaphysician among our mystics',[22] we find that although
almost startlingly original in some respects, and not least
in his methods, he is yet the heir of all the preceding
centuries. Compared with many earlier mystical writers,
his output was small, never meant for publication, and, in
a sense, almost accidental. He wrote with the practical aim
of helping souls in need, and his experience had shown
him that such need existed. And by excellence, he is the
Mystical Doctor. Previous saints and Doctors of the Church
had been mystics, and had written upon the subject, but
we have to seek their mystical teaching in their works
upon theology in general. John's four larger books, the
little 'booklets', and few surviving letters, are concerned
with spiritual theology only, if we except a few business
letters. Nor does he go over ground already adequately
covered. His friars could find all the traditional teaching

---

[19] *Letters of St. Teresa*, vol. III, n. 258, to M. Anne of Jesus. (Trs. by
the Benedictines of Stanbrook Abbey. Baker, London.)
[20] *Ibid.*, n. 259, to the same.
[21] *Ibid.*, n. 260, to M. Anne of St. Albert.
[22] Sainz-Rodriguez.

elsewhere; his task was to develop and explain matters in that teaching which had never yet been made thoroughly clear. On his own showing, he wrote for a very limited 'public': 'certain persons in our Order', whom we know were the inmates of the small, fervent Discalced Carmels of both sexes; in particular, the nuns of Beas and Granada, in Andalusia, where several of the vocations were of his fostering. Of course, his works became the common property of all the Discalced, and he did not refuse to train layfolk. The *Living Flame of Love*—hardly a book for a beginner or a dilettante!—was written for Doña Ana de Peñalosa; the *Spiritual Canticle* he wrote for Mother Anne of Jesus, foundress of both the convents mentioned. In contrast to some of his predecessors, even Denis the Carthusian who also wrote for nuns, he did not think it necessary to remind them of the weaknesses of their sex, and spiritual inferiority to men. John asked only that a soul be in earnest; that being so, he would go to any length in spending himself and being spent. Would that Teresa had been so aided in youth!

Some consideration of the tradition of the Order is called for. The word 'eclectic' has been applied to Carmel, in respect to both its dogmatic theology and its spirituality. All who are interested in the subject know something of the origin of the Reform, the bitter opposition of the Calced friars, and the sufferings of John and Teresa. But as we know also, troubles and parties arose even among the Reformed, and although these were partly due to incompatible characters, such as Fathers Jerome Gracian and Nicholas Doria, some of the trouble dated from older days.

From the first, the history of the Order had been unique. The Primitive, or rather the first Rule drawn up for the religious of Mount Carmel by Albert of Vercelli, Patriarch of Jerusalem in 1210, and found, at least in substance, in the *Institution of the First Monks*, envisaged a strictly contemplative and eremetical life, and the houses

in Palestine, like the *Deserts*[23] founded later in Europe,
were designed for an observance akin to that of the Carthusians and Camaldolese. When, after the collapse of the
Christian power in the East, the hermits drifted back to
Europe between 1241 and 1254, they eventually adopted
the status of a Mendicant Order, but never seem to have
really assimilated the spirit. At first there was strong
opposition to higher studies in the Order, during the
generalates of Nicholas the Frenchman (1265-1271) and
his successor, Ralph Alemannus, but after 1274 a broader
spirit prevailed, not least among the English friars, and in
that same year the Order, in its newer form, was finally
approved by Innocent IV, at the second Council of Lyons.
There were no Carmelite nuns until 1452, when the General, Blessed John Soreth, founded them in Guelders, and
elsewhere in the Low Countries, whence they spread to
Italy and Spain. The Rule approved for Europe, though
austere, was subsequently mitigated and it was that same
Rule, as originally formulated, which was known as the
Primitive one to which the Discalced returned.

After the embargo upon the university studies was
removed, Carmelites are found at Paris, Oxford, Cambridge,
Bologna and elsewhere, and among them were brilliant
men. They were usually Thomists, and as time went on
become 'body and soul under the banner of St. Thomas',
but their most conspicuous scholar, the Englishman, John
Baconthorpe, has been called 'the betrayer of Scholasticism!'
He certainly was eclectic and held diverging views on
several points. He was deeply interested in the Arabian
philosophers, and a specialist on Averróes, but he also
wrote an *Exposition on Mystical Theology*, and was quite
in favour of the strongly contemplative tradition in the
Order. He was still prescribed for study in the time of
St. John, and just occasionally we note a faint trace of his

---

[23] See *Les Déserts du Carmel*, by R. F. Benedict Zimmerman (Desclée). The same Carmelite scholar has written an account of the
higher studies in the Order, and the Carmelites at the universities.

views in the latter's works. Evidently St. Thomas was not yet quite master of the field when John of St. Mathias was sent to Salamanca.

As regards their spirituality, also, the Carmelites borrowed from more than one school. We know that St. John's works were attacked after his death, and in 1590, when the *Instruction of Novices* was approved, it contained a method of prayer which is decidedly elaborate, and owes not a little to the period of the *devotio moderna*, as well as to earlier authorities. The man who had been praised—and blamed—for it was the Venerable John of Jesus-Mary (Arvalles), one of the first novices of Pastrana, which was the first noviciate of the Discalced friars; but although, as a Consultor, St. John of the Cross signed it with the others, it is hard to imagine him forcing it upon anybody! At that period, however, it behoved the Reform to walk warily, and not to seem revolutionary.

In the *Institution of the first monks*, it had been laid down: 'All are called to prayer and contemplation'. 'What we obtain by our labour, with the grace of God, is to offer to God a holy heart, free from all actual stain of sin. We attain this when we are perfect in charity.' Except when in choir, the religious are required 'to remain in their cells, or near them, meditating day and night on the law of the Lord, and watching in prayer'. In their early days, the Carmelites meant by 'contemplation' just what the traditional authors meant. St. Teresa advised her daughters to 'converse with God without fatiguing the understanding',[24] and reminds them that 'love matters rather than thoughts',[25] and that progress in prayer consists not in thinking much but in loving much'.[26] When, at Segovia, John found Sister Mariana of the Cross on the point of giving up mental prayer, because for years she had experienced only dryness in her efforts to 'make meditations', he simply bade her give up

[24] *Life*, c. 8, n. 5.
[25] *Foundations*, c. 5.
[26] *Int. Castle*, M. IV.

the useless strain, and directed her, with marked success, along simpler and more spontaneous lines. Mother Mary of Jesus, at Beas, was a similar case, who had suffered much at the hands of confessors but rather grew worse, until she met the Saint, who dealt with her according to her need.

The method of Aravalles, who later became the first novice-master of the Italian Province, divides prayer into seven parts: preparation, reading, meditation, contemplation, thanksgiving, petition and epilogue. Seemingly it was meant as a compromise to satisfy all parties, and be a combination of old and new. Preparation means the remote preparation; then follows the old *lectio divina*, and the traditional meditation thereon. This leads to the simplified, but still active prayer called 'contemplation' in tradition, and which among the Discalced really meant what we ordinarily call affective prayer.

Personally Aravalles objects to using the word 'contemplation' too early, and says he means by it an application of the will to the subject, after the understanding has done its work; he also calls it an affective colloquy with God. Poor Fr. Jerome Gracian, also in that first noviciate, and no less fervent, says contemplation is an interior 'savour', or 'light'—*gusto o luz interior*—so it seems as though they were trying to make the best of the 'strait jacket' type of method, and yet remain faithful to their first novice master! Says Aravalles: 'Spiritual writers are found who mention contemplation among the parts of the mental prayer; this is a stumbling-block to beginners...they force themselves to contemplate, lose their time, and ordinarily the whole fruit of their prayer.'[27] In practice, St. John was as particular that a soul should not stop meditation too soon, as he was that it should not be forced to keep to it too long.

All traditional ascetic discipline the Saint accepts. He does not treat of meditation, simply because his readers knew all about it. Indeed, he thought some of them had had more than enough! They must aim at humility,

---

[27] *De Partibus orationis in communi. Opera omnia*, t. II.

self-knowledge and utter detachment. The way up the mountain is Christ: 'As I have said, Christ is the way, and this way is death for our natural selves, in things both of sense and spirit. I will now explain how we are to die, following the example of Christ.'[28] But John is a superb psychologist, and unique in the way in which he applies his philosophical gifts to the problems of the spiritual life.

Others had written at length about self-abnegation, and the necessity that the soul's will should be thus made one with that of God, if the highest union with Him were to be attained, but John goes into detail and gives reasons for his thoroughgoing and all-embracing requirements. Also, he shows that many people think they have achieved this union who, in reality, have still a long way to go. He has often frightened readers who tend to forget that he was writing for generous folk, 'pilgrims of the absolute', who were beginners only in the mystical way, but were already living hard, self-denying lives and aiming at much more than barely saving their souls; people who had the merciless logic of saints and children! So many are detached from so much, yet he shows them how they still retain subtle attachments; whereas if they want the All—*todo*—which is God, they must be attached to nothing—*nada*. The bird tied by a string on its leg is as effectually tethered as though the bond were a strong rope: the point is it cannot fly![29]

He explains how 'two contraries (even as philosophy teaches us) cannot exist in one person; and that darkness which is affection for creatures, and light which is God, are contrary to each other, and have no likeness or accord between one another.'[30]

Again: 'The union and transformation in God ... comes to pass when the two wills ... namely that of the soul and that of God, are conformed in one; and there is nothing in the one that is repugnant to the other.... Nothing will

---

[28] *Ascent*, B. II, c. 7, n. 9.
[29] *Ibid.*, B. I, c. 2, n. 4.
[30] *Ascent*, B. I, c. 4, n. 21.

then remain in the soul that is not the will of God, and it will thus be transformed in God.'[31] Above all, evangelical perfection—and he is writing especially for religious—means 'spoliation and emptiness of sense and spirit.'[32]

But there remained a serious problem. As a result of his experience with souls, he had found, as he tells us very frankly, that many excellent people, not least women, who were resolved to aim at sanctity, and to be generous with God, were all too often bereft of necessary guidance, forced to pray in a manner completely unsuited to them, discouraged and fearful where there was no reason for being so, and not rarely, in their doubt and bewilderment, ended by losing their ideals. At the best, they settled into a rut and made no progress, at the worst they became relaxed religious; or, if they were seculars, developed into mere formalists and might easily be led to dabble in heresy or superstition.

> It is piteous to see many a one who, though his soul would fain tarry in this peace and rest of interior quiet, where it is filled with the peace and refreshment of God, take from it its interior tranquility, and lead it away to the most exterior things, and would make it return and retrace the ground it has already traversed, to no purpose; and abandon the end and goal wherein it is already reposing, for the means which have led it to the repose, which are meditations.... [33]

John was convinced that the crisis occurs when discursive meditation and affective, sensibly consoled, prayer, which for practical purposes could be treated as the conclusion of the meditation, gave place to a seemingly unaccountable aridity, and often sheer impossibility as regards praying in one's former manner. Others had noted this, but had failed to prescribe any satisfactory remedy. John knew

---

[31] *Ibid.*, B. II, c. 5, nn. 3–4.
[32] *Ibid.*, B. II, c. 5, n. 7.
[33] *Ibid.*, B. II, c. 12, nn. 8–9.

by experience, that the contemplation extolled by earlier writers did *not* normally follow on from meditation; that since the unfortunate people so tried had usually been told that such dryness was a punishment for sin, they became miserable, scrupulous and feared they were, if not lost souls, highly likely to become such; or if they had learnt that such a trial was disciplinary, and so tried to struggle on, they often lost heart at the deadly monotony, and like some of his penitents at Beas and Granada, were tempted to give up mental prayer altogether. Again, there were souls who had never been able to use their imagination much, or make compositions of place, time, etc., and, never having been taught any other form of mental prayer, had always found their prayer time wholly penitential and something suspiciously like a sheer waste of time.

For John, the key to the problem was to be found in that form of contemplation mentioned long ago by Richard of St. Victor, and touched upon by others; yet never explained, and treated—when its existence was admitted at all—as the Cinderella of spiritual theology. So he gives us his distinctly personal teaching on the *Dark Night of the Senses* and the prayer of 'loving attention', which later theologians of his, and other, Orders would call 'acquired', 'active', 'mixed' or 'beginners' contemplation', 'prayer of "simple regard"' etc.

He explains that meditation ceases to be helpful or even possible at a certain stage, simply because its work is done. The soul has received all the spiritual good which it can derive from the things of God by meditation and reason.[34]

The time has come for it to pass to another form of prayer, and this 'new' prayer contains a contemplative element, a definite actuation of the gifts of the Holy Spirit, which is, however, not perceptible to the soul that is receiving it. The latter's activity is very simple and gentle, but none the less real. There is no question of doing nothing. The soul must maintain itself in this loving attention to God, quietly repelling distractions, and

---

[34] *Ascent*, B. II, c. 14.

helping itself with an occasional aspiration, only as it finds such helpful. It no longer thinks out more or less elaborate concepts, but is content with 'a confused, general knowledge of God', which is yet far more profitable now than its former activity. God is, so to speak, taking over much more directly Himself. Nevertheless, this state may go on for years, and it *is* at times desperately dry and monotonous; hence some of the suffering experienced by the soul. Moreover, the latter now receives new light on its spiritual poverty, its sinfulness, perhaps, rather than its actual sins, and realizes that self is far from conquered. 'God leaves him in such thick darkness that he knows not whither to turn. He cannot advance a step in meditation, as he was wont, the inward sense being overwhelmed in this night, and left in such barrenness that instead of joy and sweetness in spiritual exercises... he now finds only insipidity and bitterness.'[35] We know from the celebrated Fray Joseph of Jesus-Mary Quiroga, who was trained by those whom the Saint himself had trained, that in the noviciate John had taught 'a contemplation which we can practise with the help of our personal efforts, with the aid of the light of faith and that of ordinary grace.'[36]

But there must be no mistake in recognizing that the time has really come for this change of prayer, and here John applies the three tests found in the *Institutions* of Tauler. (1) Meditation has become impossible. (2) The soul feels no desire to practise it, even if it could, for it longs instead to be quiet with God, even though He is giving it only 'the hard crusts', as John says. (3) If it feels no sensible longing for God, it also feels none for creatures, and moreover it 'experiences in the midst of these aridities and emptiness of the faculties, a habitual care and anxiety with respect to God, together with grief

[35] *Dark Night*, c. 8.
[36] Los grados communes de la contemplación que dodemos alcanzar a nuestro modo humano, por medio de la luz de la fé y auxilio ordinários de la gracia.... (*Don que tuvo San Juan de la Cruz para guiar las almas a Dios.*)

and fear that it is not serving Him.'[37] The soul habitually
remembers God with fear and dread of backsliding upon
the spiritual road.'[38] All this shows that the trouble is
not caused by lukewarmness or temporary ill-health, and
the fact is that God has views for that soul if it is prepared to be generous and patient, carrying out its own
active purification and suffering the *passive* purification
wrought by Him. John lays it down that if the aridity is
merely intermittent, alternating with facility and sensible
sweetness, it is only disciplinary as others have thought.
The length of this *Dark Night* depends upon how much
imperfection there is to destroy, and the degree of union
with Himself to which God means to raise the soul.[39]

He explains the theology of the matter, which no one,
again, had yet done satisfactorily. Others, not least St.
Bonaventure, had emphasized at length the part played
in man's sanctification by the Theological Virtues, but
John shows how the work of detaching the soul not only
from created things, but even from spiritual good things,
and God's own gifts, which, good as they are, are yet
not God, is wrought precisely by the virtues of Faith,
Hope and Charity. The soul has to learn to live wholly
by faith, and not by sensible consolation, and that faith
enables it to walk undismayed in the darkness because it
believes in a dawn. It will not attach any importance to
visions, revelations and extraordinary graces generally—
and John is even more strongly against these than many
of his predecessors, though none of the latter failed to
warn their disciples not to desire them—for it wills only
to walk by faith in this world. Hope urges the soul to
forget the things that are behind; hence, it disciplines
its memory and never gives way to dreaming, and longs
for and presses on to the goal of union with God. The
love of God takes increasing possession of it, until a day

---

[37] *Dark Night*, B. I, c. 11, n. 2.
[38] *Ascent*, B. I, c. 13, n. 4.
[39] *Dark Night*, B. I, c. 14, n. 5.

comes when it loves nothing save in Him, but all men
for love of Him.

So, if God sees fit, He may grant the grace of infused
contemplation—mystical prayer in the strictest sense—or
Prayer of Quiet when, instead of the prayer of dry faith
and loving attention, the soul will have an experimental
knowledge of Him, and, as says St. Teresa, there will be
times when it can have no doubt whatever that it has been
with Him. At first this may occur only intermittently, and
never for long, but, always granting that the soul never
flags in its ascetic work—for it takes a long time to get
rid of all those imperfections of which we read in Tauler,
and at greater length still in John himself—or its fidelity
to prayer, this contemplation may be expected to increase
in degree and frequency. We need not treat at length of
the higher states of prayer, since the Saint's treatment of
them is in the great tradition; but as he is often called
'the Doctor of the Night', a further remark is called for.

When the first Night is passed, there usually follows a
long time in the Illuminative Way, but God is Master of
His graces and not all souls are treated alike. John tells
us that he describes the highest favours, but that not all
receive them. St. Teresa the Great was granted a plenitude
of mystical favours; St. Teresa of Lisieux was not. He
warns his readers, however, that after this period of peace
and joy, now and then there will be 'token and heralds'
of the *Night of the Spirit*, which will come in some form,
should God will to raise the soul to the state of union.[40]
In this connection, he gives a valuable reminder. Souls
suffer intensely, owing to the fact that when the *Night*
shuts down they receive no help from recalling their past
periods of spiritual happiness, and again the saint gives a
psychological explanation. 'Spiritual joys have the property
of excluding their contraries; hence the soul, when in
joy, thinks its trials will never recur, but when that joy
passes it is plunged again in the bitterness of seeming

---

[40] *Dark Night*, B. II, c. 1, n. 1.

abandonment by God. The actual presence of one thing in the mind, is naturally inconsistent with the presence and sense of its contrary.'[41]

Much has been written, by less wise persons, of John's 'inhuman' demands. He has been called 'the Doctor of the *Nada*', compared with oriental holy men, aiming at a spiritual Nirvana, etc. Such criticisms are shallow, and show the critics have not really studied him. He was a Spaniard; he had known great suffering, and supremely, he had understood the meaning of the crucifix! *That I may know Him . . . and the fellowship of His sufferings.*[42] Moreover, he had a very rich command of language in which to express that meaning. When we study 'the whole John', however, we find a most lovable personality and everything falls into place.

He never means to crush outright human affections; only affection which is 'out of order', in that it is giving God only second place. He dearly loved his mother, Catalina Alvarez, that valiant woman whose love match with the high-born and wealthy Gonzalo de Yepes had meant love in a cottage, early widowhood, and grinding poverty for her and her children, added to the enmity of her husband's family. He once introduced his brother, Francisco, as 'my brother, whom I love better than anyone in the world'. Between him and the Mother Teresa, as between him and others of his spiritual children, there existed a friendship wholly 'in Christ'. His letters always show an exquisite courtesy and kindness, and we catch glimpses of his intercourse with his brethren and sisters in religion which are idylls. Those who bore witness in his cause of Beatification, who could speak from experience, constantly emphasize his kindness and patience with everyone with whom he came into contact. His love of nature made him akin to St. Francis of Assisi, and we read how he used to take his novices on long walks into the country, or over the hills, and scatter them about

---

[41] *Ibid.*, B. II, c. 7.
[42] Phil. 3:10.

to pray. He loved to hide himself in a natural cave in a corner of the garden of the priory of Calvario, for the same purpose, and Anne of Jesus and her nuns used to call him 'God's goldfinch'. But he was in earnest and wrote for those who were likewise. To him and to them, as to every man and woman who is given a religious vocation, it was a question of: *If thou wilt be perfect!* ... *Are* you really determined to strive for sanctity? Then, says John, you must face the fact that it is a lifelong process, and that He to whom you dedicate your future life warned you that you must take up your cross daily and follow Him. 'Who seeks not the cross of Christ, seeks not the glory of Christ', he writes in his *Maximus*; and when a day comes when, like Thomas Aquinas centuries before, he is divinely commended and bidden to name a reward for what he has done, his answer is still perfectly consistent: *'Lord, to suffer and be despised for Thy sake!'*

And the reward will be exceeding great, and all which the soul's child's mistake fancied as lost will be found again, safely stored up for it. 'The perfect spiritual life, which is the possession of God through the union of love; and this is attained through the complete mortification of all the vices and desires, and of the soul's entire nature.'[43] Words fail John, as they must do every other mystic, when he tries to describe what that reward will be, even in this life; and so it must be, for no tongue or words can express what is inexpressible even for one who has known it from experience! We may end on his own exultant outburst:

The heavens are mine, the earth is mine, and the peoples are mine! Mine are the just and the sinners are mine: mine are the angels and the Mother of God is mine! All things are mine! God Himself is mine and for me, because Christ is mine and all for me![44]

---

[43] *Living Flame*, c. 2, n. 28.
[44] *Spiritual Maximus and Sentences*, 25.

INDEX TO PERSONS

www.ingramcontent.com/pod-product-compliance
Lightning Source LLC
Chambersburg PA
CBHW030300130626
46549CB00002B/626